PLATO

THE MARTYRDOM
OF SOCRATES

Edited with Introduction,
Notes and Vocabulary by

F.C. Doherty

Bristol Classical Press

Cover illustration: *The Death of Socrates*, etching after the painting
by Jacques-Louis David (1787) now in the Metropolitan Museum, New York.

First published by Oxford University Press in 1923

Reprinted 1981, 1996, 1997, 2001 by
Bristol Classical Press
an imprint of
Gerald Duckworth & Co. Ltd
61 Frith Street
London W1D 3JL
e-mail: inquiries@duckworth-publishers.co.uk
Website: www.ducknet.co.uk

A catalogue record for this book is available
from the British Library

ISBN 0-906515-96-3

Printed in Great Britain by
Antony Rowe Ltd, Eastbourne

NOTE

I DESIRE to express my obligation to the authorities of Balliol College, Oxford, and to the Clarendon Press, for permission to make use of Jowett's translation : to the Warden of Radley College, to Mr. C. Bailey, and to Mr. R. W. Livingstone for much invaluable advice and criticism, and to my colleague, Mr. H. H. S. Wright, for assistance in checking the vocabulary.

F. C. D.

INTRODUCTION

OF the death of Socrates it has been written : 'There is nothing in any tragedy, ancient or modern, nothing in poetry or history, like the last hours of Socrates in Plato.' Several accounts of the closing scenes of his life have come down to us, but the purpose of this book is to study only that of Plato, his disciple and ardent admirer. The tragedy itself falls into three acts. The first of these, contained in the *Apology*, comprises the three speeches made by Socrates at his trial. The second consists of the dialogue known as the *Crito*, which took place between him and his old friend Crito in the prison where, after his condemnation, he awaited the execution of the death-sentence. The third, in which we read the story of his last hours and death, is taken from the *Phaedo*, one of the greatest masterpieces in the literature of the ancient world.

In all these works Plato without doubt intended to exhibit his master to posterity in the noblest light; he writes as an artist to whom his art and purpose are paramount, and to some extent perhaps he subordinates historical accuracy to other considerations. In his works we learn to know Socrates as Plato wished the world to know him. Yet in actual fact he is probably but little removed from the real Socrates.

It is always possible to correct and supplement our first estimate by later reading; in the meantime for many reasons it is no small thing to know him 'according to Plato'. In the first place nobody can come into contact with this extraordinary man without feeling in some way the better for it: the spell which he cast over so many of his contemporaries, especially in their youth, has lost little of its magic with the passage of over two thousand years. Secondly, he is the earliest exponent of the scientific spirit of the modern world which seeks Truth by the light of reason as an end worth pursuing for its own sake. He also foreshadowed long before their time many of the ideals of the religion upon which we claim to base our civilization to-day. Finally, his death was that of a martyr, a fact which has set the seal of romance upon his name, though indeed apart from this he would have remained an outstanding figure in history for his indomitable courage, high principles, and sincerity of conviction.

II. THE STAGE AND ITS SETTING

We must begin by getting as clear an idea as possible of the stage upon which this drama was enacted, and of its setting. Socrates was put to death in 399 B.C., being then seventy years old. His early manhood coincides with the time at which his native city of Athens reached the zenith of her greatness, and his maturity and old age with that of the beginning of her decline.

In the early part of the fifth century she had stood forth as the champion of the smaller Greek states in their struggle for liberty against the Persian invaders, who represented orientalism and the principle of a vast united empire. Such a principle was instinctively abhorred by the Greeks. They dwelt around the coasts and in the islands of the Aegean in small communities, geographically isolated, each free and self-governing, actively resenting any interference with their institutions. Of these Athens herself is by far the most interesting, and of her our knowledge is most complete. Her inhabitants were a maritime people, hardy, quick-witted, and intelligent, eager to work out their salvation in their own state, for in its constitution they felt, both as individuals and as a people, that they could secure the most real happiness and the best life.

After the Persian threat had been removed by the brilliant victories of Salamis and Plataea, Athens found herself the natural leader of those states which had, during the great emergency, united to vindicate the principles of freedom against those of empire and arbitrary government. The communities to which Persia was most likely to be a danger still were those of the sea-board and islands, and among them was formed the Confederacy of Delos, a league which was to maintain a navy large enough to hold the ancient enemy in check, if not to indemnify the Greek losses in the late wars by carrying hostilities into the enemy's country. Partly, however, by force of circumstances, partly by design, the whole organization fell into Athenian hands and became the basis of the new Athenian Empire. The change took place so gradually that the Greek world hardly awoke to it until it was an accomplished fact. The fleet which had been the common property of the league became in Athenian hands an instrument for coercing its unruly members, while its funds went to glorify the imperial city with the magnificent buildings which were to make her worthy of her position as the centre of the Greek world.

The greatness of Athens did not last long. The inevitable jealousy of her neighbours, especially those whose constitutions were not democratic, and the discontent of the subject-states, whose liberty had been sacrificed to create what now appeared to them little short of a tyranny, brought upon her the Peloponnesian War (431 B.C.). The long-drawn struggle sapped her vitality. The plague reduced the numbers of her fighting men, and constant expeditions the resources of her treasury. Her brilliant scheme of a western empire collapsed with the disastrous failure of the Sicilian expedition (415 B.C.). There was internal strife. The wisdom of Pericles was succeeded by the folly of unscrupulous party politicians and violent demagogues, and even by open treachery like that of Alcibiades. In 404 B.C. came her final humiliation and the installation of oligarchical government under the Thirty Tyrants, led by Critias and backed by the power of Sparta. It is true that after a short ten months, crowded with excesses of the most violent kind, the democracy was restored, but neither Athens nor indeed Greece herself recovered from the effects of the previous thirty years.

Such in bare outline is the history of his city during the lifetime of Socrates; it must be borne in mind while we consider him, for it had an inevitable reaction upon the minds of the Athenian people, and it is with them that he was concerned. From 450 B.C. onwards the Athenians are an imperial people, enjoying an assured position and the leisure which their new-found wealth and prosperity have brought them, and intensely interested in the concrete problem of making a success of life. Their constitution is democratic, and every man is forced to realize his responsibilities as a citizen: he serves his time in the army and takes his turn as a juryman in the law-courts, he votes in the Assembly, where questions of peace and war and of the making of treaties are decided, and is at some time or other a member of the Council of Five Hundred, which is practically the governing body in the state. Every man is first and foremost a politician, and whether he enjoys the advantages of birth and wealth, or whether he makes a scanty living out of his goats upon the mountains, the highest offices of the state are open to him. For success of this kind, however, his education does little to fit him; it gives him a knowledge of reading and writing, teaches him something of the laws of his country and of its early literature, and equips him for feats of physical endurance— but there it ends. A demand arose for what we should call university education, and since demand generally creates supply, there appeared a class of professional teachers, known to the world as the sophists, who were prepared in exchange for money to impart knowledge on every conceivable subject, and above all on the art of managing one's affairs and making a success of life. They moved from place to place as they found a market for their wares, and nowhere was such a market to be found as at Athens.

It is worth while to consider some of them a little more closely. One of the most famous is perhaps Protagoras of Abdera, who spent much of his life at Athens. He claimed to teach men to deliberate wisely both about their own affairs and those of the state, and to take their part, whether in speech or action, in public life. He is said to have been prepared to argue either side of any question, and to show men 'how to make the weaker argument prevail', while about the gods he was not prepared either to affirm or to deny their existence. Gorgias of Leontini in Sicily was one of the most famous teachers of rhetoric, and specialized in the study of style—alliteration, metaphor, antithesis, and all the other subtleties of the professional orator, with which Plato finds fault on the ground that men are led thereby to believe what is not true. Prodicus, from the island of Ceos, who professed to be a teacher of virtue, pronounced what must have seemed to conservative opinion the dangerous doctrine that the gods were personifications by man of what was most beneficial to him in life. Our last example, Hippias of Elis, is distinguished for his versatile nature : he was a rhetorician who, besides teaching the art of politics, studied astronomy, wrote poetry, invented a system of memory-training, and even appeared once at Olympia in elaborate attire, every article of which he claimed to have made with his own hands.

Such were the men from whom, at fees ranging from £20 to £200 a course, the new generation of imperial Athenians obtained their higher education. They were acutely interested in all the problems of practical politics and practical morality, and took to the new learning like

ducks to water. They practised their attainments and
sharpened their critical faculties in endless conversation
upon every subject under the sun, and in due course discovered that in all spheres, including that of religion, what
had been good enough for their fathers was not good
enough for them. The morality of the Olympian gods as
depicted in the Homeric legends began to be called in
question. Though the official state-worship, with its cere-
monial of procession and sacrifice, theatrical performance
and athletic contest, proved satisfactory as an external
expression of their experiences in the world, it offered no
basis for a personal religion, the need of which was now
beginning to be felt, as the cults of the Eleusinian and
Orphic mysteries show.

This revolutionary atmosphere of criticism and doubt,
discussion and argument, is the immediate setting of the
drama which we have to study.

III. The Central Figure

Upon this stage and in this setting moved Socrates, the
man with a mission. His outward appearance alone would
have marked him out from among his fellows as belonging
to an unusual type. Short and strongly built, with a snub
nose, thick lips, and rather prominent eyes, frankly ugly,
going barefoot save on important occasions, and always
wearing the plainest of clothes, he was the reverse of all
that the Athenians admired in the way of beauty. In spite,
however, of this unattractive exterior, which caused his
friends to liken him to a Silenus or a satyr, there were
many things about him which could not fail to excite
interest. He had a wide reputation for courage, attested
by at least two incidents in his military career. In the
Peloponnesian War, during the siege of Potidaea, he had
saved the life of Alcibiades, and when the latter demanded
that he should receive the prize for valour, had waived his
claim in favour of his brilliant friend and admirer. Again,

in the hour of disaster at Delium, he was distinguished by his presence of mind and self-possession amid the panic which overtook the rest of the Athenian army.

Besides this there was more than an air of mystery about him. Men said that he was subject to strange trances, and told how, on a famous occasion at Potidaea, he had gone out of camp in the early morning to think over some problem, and had stood motionless in rapt meditation for the space of twenty-four hours, so that some of his fellow-soldiers even spent the night in the open, so anxious were they to see how long this fit of abstraction would last. There could have been few who had not heard of the 'divine sign', as Socrates called it, the mysterious voice which from his childhood onward had come to him from time to time, compelling him to refrain from some intended action. Such was the man who haunted the market-places and colonnades of Athens, spending his days in ceaseless conversation, not only with his friends and acquaintances, but with any man, whether Athenian or foreigner, who had the leisure and inclination to listen.

The origin and nature of his mission, as well as his method of pursuing it, are fully described in the *Apology*. The Delphic oracle told his friend Chaerephon that Socrates was the wisest man in the world. Socrates, famous for a sense of humour and of the fitness of things, set out to prove the oracle wrong by finding some one wiser than himself. In the end, after long and earnest investigation, he was forced to admit that the reply of Apollo was true in a certain sense: no man, he concluded, was truly wise, but he himself was superior to the rest of mankind in that he was not wise and knew it, whereas they were not wise and yet thought that they were. He therefore regarded the words of the oracle as a direct command to spend his life in trying to make his fellow-men realize for themselves what he had discovered in his own case, and abandon their pretensions to wisdom, for until they had done so, he held that they could not aspire to true wisdom or true knowledge. He freely criticized their ideas, their actions, and their institutions, and thus he resembled many of the leaders of the new thought, but with this difference, that while they criticized from sheer love of destruction, he destroyed in order to obtain a solid foundation on which to rebuild. The Old Testament prophets spent their days in convincing men of sin; Socrates spent his in convincing them of ignorance. Yet in his eyes ignorance was sin. He always insisted that just as a craftsman who has a thorough knowledge of his art cannot fail to produce the object of it, so a man who has right knowledge cannot fail to perform right actions.

This knowledge, which was to replace the prevailing ignorance, was the knowledge enjoined by the famous γνῶθι σεαυτόν inscribed on the walls of Apollo's temple at Delphi, the knowledge of a man's true self and the things that belong to it. It was the knowledge of a man's capacities and limitations, of that part of him which cannot be satisfied with riches, power, and honour, but only with the treasure laid up in heaven. He tried, as he tells us, to persuade men to care for their souls first, and for success in life afterwards; and herein lies his claim to be considered the apostle of a new age. Before his time the soul, except to the initiates of the Orphic mysteries, had been at best a shadowy thing, unconvincing and of little worth beside the concrete, visible activities and enjoyments of everyday life, to which the Greeks had always attached so much value. He was in fact among the first to proclaim the ultimate worth of the human soul, a theory which lies behind our modern ideas of the brotherhood of mankind. So he maintained continually that the only thing which really merits all the thought and trouble so freely lavished on other things by man is that part of a man which is concerned with what is good and bad, right and wrong, just and unjust.

His method was a simple one, and of this too he speaks in the *Apology*. He made it his business in the first place to try to remove all the erroneous ideas which had become so prevalent, especially since the old traditional view of life and morals had been challenged by the new school of thought. All his teaching was conducted by means of conversation, the 'dialectic' method of question and answer, a method peculiarly suited to his age, when argument was the order of the day. A chance discussion would lead to the mention of goodness, justice, freedom, or some similar word which was upon every man's tongue. Socrates usually made a start by demanding a definition, and it would soon become apparent that his companion had a very unsatisfactory notion of defining his subject, as was natural in an age when men spent more time in talking than in thinking about the matter of their talk. Driven from one attempt to another by the remorseless cross-examination of Socrates, the unfortunate victim would end as often as not by contradicting himself. Meno, for example, says : 'I do not know how to answer you ; and though I have delivered an infinite variety of speeches about virtue before now, and to many persons—and very good ones they were, as I thought—at this moment I cannot even say what virtue is.' (*Meno* 80 A.)

This feeling of helplessness was, in the eyes of Socrates, a necessary preliminary to any advance on the road to knowledge. All his associates had first to learn the folly of their former 'wisdom' ; this can only be done in a spirit of humility, and humility was a commodity as rare then as it is now. The older men grow, the less willing they are to have their favourite ideas and prejudices violently overthrown ; hence the fact that Socrates found his following mainly among the youth of Athens. But whether young or old, the vain, the self-satisfied, the prejudiced, and the conservative among his hearers can never have endured him long enough to feel anything more than

extreme indignation and resentment. Such no doubt
were the majority; only the few remained to hear him
suggesting other ways of reaching a conclusion. It
was not his way to solve the problem he had raised,
for he realized the limited nature of his own knowledge. Rather he contented himself with drawing from
the daily life around him examples which seemed to
have a bearing on the question, and with trying to find
some general rule or principle which would cover the
facts. So familiar were his illustrations that in one place
it is said that his conversation was all 'of pack-asses and
smiths and cobblers and curriers'. But though his style
of speaking was humble, the effect upon his audience was
remarkable, for it produced an intellectual experience
like that which we call in terms of religion 'conversion',
the turning of the mind in a new and better direction.
In both cases subsequent progress depends on individual
effort, and it is partly because he grasped this and partly
because he felt that men can only see 'through a glass
darkly' that he preferred to suspend judgement rather than
to dogmatize.

To illustrate the effect of his words we may take the
testimony of Alcibiades. 'I have heard Pericles and
other great orators, and I thought that they spoke well,
but I never had any similar feeling; my soul was not
stirred by them, nor was I angry at my own slavish state.'
And again: 'He makes me confess that I ought not to
live as I do, neglecting the wants of my own soul and
busying myself with the concerns of the Athenians.'
(*Symposium* 215–16.) It is true that Alcibiades did not
listen in the end to any voice save that of his own
ambition, but the effect upon him is obvious, and it is
caused by more than mere words. There was a peculiar
charm about the personality of Socrates which exercised
an almost magnetic influence upon his friends, and
especially upon the young, for he was completely in

sympathy with the spirit of adventure in which they regard life. Alcibiades is our witness again. 'I hold my ears and tear myself away from him,' he says; 'many a time have I wished that he were dead, and yet I know that I should be much more sorry than glad if he were to die: so that I am at my wits' end.' In the same place he says: 'Your words amaze and possess the souls of every man, woman, and child who comes within hearing of them. .. My heart leaps within me and my eyes rain tears when I hear them.' (*Symposium* 215.)

If this then is a picture of Socrates the critic and teacher, what was the cause of his trial and his tragic end at the hands of the public executioner?

IV. His Opponents

A man of revolutionary ideas, however peaceful, is never in want of enemies. We learn from his defence that those of Socrates fell into two classes, the old and the new, and we must examine both in order to find an ex-planation for his condemnation and execution.

He himself takes Aristophanes as an instance of the first class. In the *Clouds*, produced in 423 B. C., we have a caricature of a Socrates who studies natural science, regards the clouds as deities, and swears by such strange gods as Air, Respiration, and Chaos; he conducts a school where his disciples are trained in outlandish ways of thinking, and the central scene is a contest between the Just and the Unjust Arguments as to which is better fitted for the education of young men, concluding with the inevitable victory of the latter. It is possible that nobody regarded the *Clouds* as being much more than a burlesque at the time, aimed generally at the sophists, of whom Aristophanes rather unfairly chose Socrates as an example. But neither the victim nor his friends took the trouble to contradict it, and the charge of atheism contained in it may well have found an echo in the minds of his judges so long afterwards. There seems to be some foundation for the caricature in the fact that when it was written Socrates was looking to the natural science of the Ionians for a solution of the problems of life ; but he abandoned it in favour of his new quest just about the time of the play's production.

The second class is represented by the men who actually brought him to trial. Of these, Meletus was a tragic poet, young, obscure, and of unattractive appear-ance, while of Lycon we know little, except that he was a rhetorician. Anytus, however, the moving spirit in the prosecution, was a man of very different calibre. He was one of the acknowledged champions of the restored democracy, and a leading political figure at Athens at this time. He had taken part in the recent exile, and was a man whose courage and strong political convictions did not prevent him from showing a noble generosity to his enemies in the hour of their defeat. He had already had dealings with Socrates, to whose company his son was strongly drawn. Anytus did his best to prevent the asso-ciation, on the ground that the philosopher was known to disapprove of democratic principles. Socrates replied by saying that a man of his position ought not to bring his son up to his father's trade, which was that of a tanner. Torn between the two, the young man fell from indecision and unhappiness to the level of a confirmed drunkard, for whose ruin Anytus no doubt held Socrates responsible. It is easy to understand his reasons for believing that Socrates and his teaching were in part at least the cause of the diseases from which Athens seemed to him to be suffering.

Such were the men who undertook the prosecution. The indictment contained a twofold charge. It stated in the first place that Socrates did not believe in the gods of the state, but introduced new gods, and in the second that he corrupted the youth. With regard to the first, he was

probably no less unorthodox than many thinkers of his
time. He always urged that men should follow the
custom of their country in the worship of the gods, and
we know that he had a lively faith in oracles. If he
criticized the Homeric legends of the gods, did not Aristophanes himself introduce Dionysus as the central figure
in his *Frogs*, and bring him into a number of ridiculous
situations? If, on the other hand, this part of the accusation was more particularly directed against the δαιμόνιον,
or 'divine sign', Socrates certainly never claimed that
this was anything more than a kind of prophetic faculty,
vouchsafed to him by the gods. Such a charge, however,
is extremely difficult to answer, and he was certainly
unfortunate in the method he chose. He dealt with it by
means of a skilful cross-examination in which he involved
Meletus in a contradiction, but his reply was nothing more
or less than a pure piece of dialectics, thoroughly in keep-
ing with sophistic methods, and for that reason probably
calculated to annoy an honest juror. It cannot be considered by any means an adequate attempt to refute this
part of the indictment.

    To the charge of corrupting the youth, which was far
the more important of the two, especially when we consider the state of political feeling in Athens at this period,
Socrates could only reply by offering to allow the friends
and relatives of the young men with whom he associated
to give evidence against him, if they desired to do so.
There can be little doubt that many young men who
chiefly consorted with him were far more ready to imitate
his methods of criticism, especially when directed against
the ideas and institutions of their fathers, than to take
to heart the high ideals of life which their teacher set
before them both in theory and practice. Those who did
not know him personally may never have realized at all
that he had such ideals. Lack of respect for the older
generation, criticism of the established order, and a marked

inclination towards oligarchy—all these things must have seemed to the Athenians sure signs of corruption in his followers.

It was well known, moreover, that Socrates did not approve of democratic methods of government. He held that politics was an exact art and that politicians ought to be experts and specialists, a view not easily reconciled with a system of annual magistracies and the use of the lot. This no doubt was the true reason for his abstention from politics, an attitude unintelligible to the ordinary Athenian, to whom it was the serious business of life. It has been said too that Chaerephon was the only one of his associates who was a true admirer of democracy, the rest in varying degrees were of oligarchical sympathies, while Socrates himself had been heard more than once to express admiration for the constitution of the ancient enemy Sparta. Again, when the rule of the Thirty was installed, most of the popular party were either driven out of Athens or else went into voluntary exile. Socrates, however, although he refused to countenance the illegal acts of the Tyranny, remained at Athens and was not interfered with in any way. The democrats would therefore naturally regard him with suspicion, and infer that he relied on the protection of Critias, the most bitter and violent of the Thirty, who had for a long time been intimate with him. Men might well ask whether Socrates had not been responsible for the education and political views of a man whose hands were stained with the blood of many a loyal democrat. Again, they might consider the case of Alcibiades, once the brilliant leader of the Athenians, and afterwards their betrayer. Here at least was an unscrupulous young man, who had added to his other offences, among which was the profanation of the mysteries, the crowning crime of treason; and there was no one for whom Socrates had professed deeper feelings of friendship.

In face of all this it must be acknowledged that the part of the defence which relates to the actual charges sounds inadequate   The remainder of it is devoted to a general justification of the speaker's whole manner of living, and it shows that his life was singularly free from reproach of any sort. Herein lies the tragedy. It is probable that most undirected juries would have returned the same verdict. Whether he would or no, Socrates was clearly a danger to the old order. The decision for the jurors was a difficult one, and the whole story only helps to show how difficult it is to arrive at such intellectual decisions, and how easy it is from quite good motives to commit a great injustice.

It remains to consider the largely increased majority in favour of the death penalty. It is probable, as the *Crito* suggests, that Meletus and Anytus with their party would have been satisfied with something less rigorous; if, for example, Socrates had proposed banishment, they would have been content. His second speech explains the sudden increase of hostility. There can be no doubt that the judges were thoroughly roused at what they considered to be his flagrant contempt of court. His refusal to make any appeal, his half-humorous irony and complete indifference to the consequences of his words signed his death-warrant.

V. Conclusion

The life and death of Socrates mark a definite stage in the progress of human thought. Hitherto the most important influence in men's lives had been the community to which they belonged. The Greeks, in the very forefront of civilization, fighting for existence not only against barbarism, but against the forces of nature themselves, were compelled to realize the political and social unity of the state. Men were citizens first, and individuals afterwards; and in accordance with this conception their lives and actions were judged. Within the state they achieved what they understood by liberty, but it was a form of liberty which only permitted the full development of the individual along certain fixed lines.

The city-state at its highest tended to mould its inhabitants to a type calculated to preserve it, and could not accommodate any other. If a man were unusual, if he thought more of his own ends than those of his city, he could find no place in the old order. Pausanias the Spartan is an early example of this sort; Pericles is another, for he only maintained his ascendancy at Athens by shrewdly identifying his city with his ambition; Alcibiades, whose genius was of that brilliant, restless kind which resists all control, conveniently sums up the type. To this class, though in a way peculiarly his own, Socrates undoubtedly belongs, but he reconciles the two aspects, for he combines thoroughly un-Greek individualism with a high sense of duty to the state. It is not his fault that his ideas and teaching were in conflict with the political system in which they were nursed. When he refused to escape from prison, he justified himself by an appeal to an entirely new principle, that it is always wrong to requite evil with evil, not so much because a man who does so injures the community, but because he injures his fellow-men as such. So far from being Greek, his argument brings us within measurable reach of the Sermon on the Mount.

Though there might be many more elaborate appreciations of him, there can be none more appropriate than that which ends the story of his last hours. 'Such was the end, Echecrates, of our friend, concerning whom I may truly say, that of all the men of his time whom I have known, he was the wisest and best.' (*Phaedo* 118.)

THE MARTYRDOM OF SOCRATES

SCENE I. THE TRIAL

FIRST SPEECH

Socrates opens his defence.

How you, O Athenians, have been affected by my accusers, I cannot tell; but I know that they almost made me forget who I was—so persuasively did they speak; and yet they have hardly uttered a word of truth. But of the many falsehoods told by them, there 5 was one which quite amazed me—I mean when they said that you should be upon your guard and not allow yourselves to be deceived by the force of my eloquence. B To say this, when they were certain to be detected as soon as I opened my lips and proved myself to be anything but a great speaker, did indeed appear to be most shameless—unless by the force of eloquence they mean 5 the force of truth ; for if such is their meaning, I admit that I am eloquent. But in how different a way from theirs !

Socrates has no experience of rhetoric, whether in the law-courts or elsewhere, and apologizes for having recourse to his usual methods of speaking.

Οὗτοι μὲν οὖν, ὥσπερ ἐγὼ λέγω, ἤ τι ἢ οὐδὲν ἀληθὲς εἰρήκασιν, ὑμεῖς δέ μου ἀκούσεσθε πᾶσαν τὴν ἀλήθειαν 10 —οὐ μέντοι μὰ Δία, ὦ ἄνδρες Ἀθηναῖοι, κεκαλλιεπη-μένους γε λόγους, ὥσπερ οἱ τούτων, ῥήμασί τε καὶ ὀνό-μασιν οὐδὲ κεκοσμημένους, ἀλλ' ἀκούσεσθε εἰκῇ λεγό- C μενα τοῖς ἐπιτυχοῦσιν ὀνόμασιν—πιστεύω γὰρ δίκαια εἶναι ἃ λέγω—καὶ μηδεὶς ὑμῶν προσδοκησάτω ἄλλως· οὐδὲ γὰρ ἂν δήπου πρέποι, ὦ ἄνδρες, τῇδε τῇ ἡλικίᾳ ὥσπερ μειρακίῳ πλάττοντι λόγους εἰς ὑμᾶς εἰσιέναι. 5

καὶ μέντοι καὶ πάνυ, ὦ ἄνδρες Ἀθηναῖοι, τοῦτο ὑμῶν
δέομαι καὶ παρίεμαι· ἐὰν διὰ τῶν αὐτῶν λόγων ἀκούητέ
μου ἀπολογουμένου δι᾽ ὧνπερ εἴωθα λέγειν καὶ ἐν ἀγορᾷ
ἐπὶ τῶν τραπεζῶν, ἵνα ὑμῶν πολλοὶ ἀκηκόασι, καὶ
D ἄλλοθι, μήτε θαυμάζειν μήτε θορυβεῖν τούτου ἕνεκα.
ἔχει γὰρ οὑτωσί. νῦν ἐγὼ πρῶτον ἐπὶ δικαστήριον
ἀναβέβηκα, ἔτη γεγονὼς ἑβδομήκοντα· ἀτεχνῶς οὖν
ξένως ἔχω τῆς ἐνθάδε λέξεως. ὥσπερ οὖν ἄν, εἰ τῷ
5 ὄντι ξένος ἐτύγχανον ὤν, συνεγιγνώσκετε δήπου ἄν μοι
18 εἰ ἐν ἐκείνῃ τῇ φωνῇ τε καὶ τῷ τρόπῳ ἔλεγον ἐν οἷσπερ
ἐτεθράμμην, καὶ δὴ καὶ νῦν τοῦτο ὑμῶν δέομαι δίκαιον,
ὥς γέ μοι δοκῶ, τὸν μὲν τρόπον τῆς λέξεως ἐᾶν—ἴσως
μὲν γὰρ χείρων, ἴσως δὲ βελτίων ἂν εἴη—αὐτὸ δὲ τοῦτο
5 σκοπεῖν καὶ τούτῳ τὸν νοῦν προσέχειν, εἰ δίκαια λέγω
ἢ μή· δικαστοῦ μὲν γὰρ αὕτη ἀρετή, ῥήτορος δὲ τἀληθῆ
λέγειν.

*His accusers are of two kinds : those who have been prejudiced
against him for a long time, and have infected others with their
prejudice, and those who have brought the case into court. He
proposes to deal with the former first.*

And first, I have to reply to the older charges and
to my first accusers, and then I will go on to the
B later ones. For of old I have had many accusers, who
have accused me falsely to you during many years ;
and I am more afraid of them than of Anytus and his
associates, who are dangerous, too, in their own way.
5 But far more dangerous are the others, who began
when you were children, and took possession of your
minds with their falsehoods, telling of one Socrates,
a wise man, who speculated about the heaven above,
and searched into the earth beneath, and made the
10 worse appear the better cause. The disseminators of
c this tale are the accusers whom I dread ; for their
hearers are apt to fancy that such inquirers do not
believe in the existence of the gods. And they are
many, and their charges against me are of ancient
date, and they were made by them in the days when

you were more impressible than you are now—in childhood, or it may have been in youth—and the cause
when heard went by default, for there was none to
answer. And hardest of all, I do not know and cannot
tell the names of my accusers; unless in the chance D
case of a Comic poet. All who from envy and malice
have persuaded you—some of them having first convinced
themselves—all this class of men are most difficult to
deal with; for I cannot have them up here, and cross- 5
examine them, and therefore I must simply fight with
shadows in my own defence, and argue when there is
no one who answers. I will ask you then to assume
with me, as I was saying, that my opponents are of two
kinds : one recent, the other ancient; and I hope that E
you will see the propriety of my answering the latter
first, for these accusations you heard long before the
others, and much oftener.

Well, then, I must make my defence, and endeavour 5
to clear away in a short time a slander which has 19
lasted a long time. May I succeed, if to succeed be
for my good and yours, or likely to avail me in my
cause! The task is not an easy one; I quite understand the nature of it. And so leaving the event with 5
God, in obedience to the law I will now make my
defence.

*He has been represented as a scientific charlatan, an accusation
for which there are no grounds.*

I will begin at the beginning, and ask what is the
accusation which has given rise to the slander of me,
and in fact has encouraged Meletus to prefer this charge B
against me. Well, what do the slanderers say? They
shall be my prosecutors, and I will sum up their words
in an affidavit : 'Socrates is an evil-doer, and a curious
person, who searches into things under the earth and 5
in heaven, and he makes the worse appear the better
cause; and he teaches the aforesaid doctrines to others.'
Such is the nature of the accusation; it is just what C
you have yourselves seen in the comedy of Aristophanes, who has introduced a man whom he calls
Socrates, going about and saying that he walks in
air, and talking a deal of nonsense concerning matters 5

of which I do not pretend to know either much or little
—not that I mean to speak disparagingly of any one
who is a student of natural philosophy. I should be
very sorry if Meletus could bring so grave a charge
10 against me. But the simple truth is, O Athenians,
that I have nothing to do with physical speculations.
D Very many of those here present are witnesses to the
truth of this, and to them I appeal. Speak then, you
who have heard me, and tell your neighbours whether
any of you have ever known me hold forth in few
5 words or in many upon such matters. . . . You hear
their answer. And from what they say of this part
of the charge you will be able to judge of the truth of
the rest.

It has been said that he teaches others and exacts payment for
his teaching: unlike the sophists, he does not profess to teach and
receives no fees.

Ἀλλὰ γὰρ οὔτε τούτων οὐδέν ἐστιν, οὐδέ γ᾽ εἴ τινος
10 ἀκηκόατε ὡς ἐγὼ παιδεύειν ἐπιχειρῶ ἀνθρώπους καὶ
E χρήματα πράττομαι, οὐδὲ τοῦτο ἀληθές. ἐπεὶ καὶ
τοῦτό γέ μοι δοκεῖ καλὸν εἶναι, εἴ τις οἷός τ᾽ εἴη παιδεύειν ἀνθρώπους ὥσπερ Γοργίας τε ὁ Λεοντῖνος καὶ
Πρόδικος ὁ Κεῖος καὶ Ἱππίας ὁ Ἠλεῖος. τούτων γὰρ
5 ἕκαστος, ὦ ἄνδρες, οἷός τ᾽ ἐστὶν ἰὼν εἰς ἑκάστην τῶν
πόλεων τοὺς νέους—οἷς ἔξεστι τῶν ἑαυτῶν πολιτῶν
προῖκα συνεῖναι ᾧ ἂν βούλωνται—τούτους πείθουσι
20 τὰς ἐκείνων συνουσίας ἀπολιπόντας σφίσιν συνεῖναι
χρήματα διδόντας καὶ χάριν προσειδέναι. ἐπεὶ καὶ
ἄλλος ἀνήρ ἐστι Πάριος ἐνθάδε σοφὸς ὃν ἐγὼ ᾐσθόμην
ἐπιδημοῦντα· ἔτυχον γὰρ προσελθὼν ἀνδρὶ ὃς τετέλεκε
5 χρήματα σοφισταῖς πλείω ἢ σύμπαντες οἱ ἄλλοι,
Καλλίᾳ τῷ Ἱππονίκου· τοῦτον οὖν ἀνηρόμην—ἐστὸν
γὰρ αὐτῷ δύο ὑεῖ—"Ὦ Καλλία," ἦν δ᾽ ἐγώ, "εἰ μέν
σου τὼ ὑεῖ πώλω ἢ μόσχω ἐγενέσθην, εἴχομεν ἂν αὐτοῖν
ἐπιστάτην λαβεῖν καὶ μισθώσασθαι ὃς ἔμελλεν αὐτὼ
B καλώ τε κἀγαθὼ ποιήσειν τὴν προσήκουσαν ἀρετήν, ἦν
δ᾽ ἂν οὗτος ἢ τῶν ἱππικῶν τις ἢ τῶν γεωργικῶν· νῦν

δ' ἐπειδὴ ἀνθρώπω ἐστόν, τίνα αὐτοῖν ἐν νῷ ἔχεις
ἐπιστάτην λαβεῖν; τίς τῆς τοιαύτης ἀρετῆς, τῆς ἀνθρω-
πίνης τε καὶ πολιτικῆς, ἐπιστήμων ἐστίν; οἶμαι γάρ σε 5
ἐσκέφθαι διὰ τὴν τῶν ὑέων κτῆσιν. ἔστιν τις," ἔφην
ἐγώ, " ἢ οὔ;" " Πάνυ γε," ἦ δ' ὅς. " Τίς," ἦν δ' ἐγώ,
" καὶ ποδαπός, καὶ πόσου διδάσκει;" " Εὔηνος," ἔφη,
" ὦ Σώκρατες, Πάριος, πέντε μνῶν." καὶ ἐγὼ τὸν
Εὔηνον ἐμακάρισα εἰ ὡς ἀληθῶς ἔχοι ταύτην τὴν 10
τέχνην καὶ οὕτως ἐμμελῶς διδάσκει. ἐγὼ γοῦν καὶ C
αὐτὸς ἐκαλλυνόμην τε καὶ ἡβρυνόμην ἂν εἰ ἠπιστάμην
ταῦτα· ἀλλ' οὐ γὰρ ἐπίσταμαι, ὦ ἄνδρες Ἀθηναῖοι.

*He can only attribute his evil reputation to the reply given to
the impetuous Chaerephon by the Delphic oracle, which pronounced him the wisest of men.*

I dare say, Athenians, that some one among you
will reply, 'Yes, Socrates, but what is the origin of 5
these accusations which are brought against you ; there
must have been something strange which you have been
doing? All these rumours and this talk about you
would never have arisen if you had been like other
men : tell us, then, what is the cause of them, for we 10
should be sorry to judge hastily of you.' Now I regard
this as a fair challenge, and I will endeavour to explain D
to you the reason why I am called wise and have such
an evil fame. Please to attend then. And although
some of you may think that I am joking, I declare
that I will tell you the entire truth. Men of Athens, 5
this reputation of mine has come of a certain sort of
wisdom which I possess. If you ask me what kind
of wisdom, I reply, wisdom such as may perhaps be
attained by man, for to that extent I am inclined to
believe that I am wise ; whereas the persons of whom 10
I was speaking have a superhuman wisdom, which I E
may fail to describe, because I have it not myself; and
he who says that I have, speaks falsely, and is taking
away my character. And here, O men of Athens,
I must beg you not to interrupt me, even if I seem to 5
say something extravagant. For the word which I will
speak is not mine. I will refer you to a witness who is

worthy of credit; that witness shall be the God of
Delphi—he will tell you about my wisdom, if I have
10 any, and of what sort it is. You must have known
21 Chaerephon; he was early a friend of mine, and also
a friend of yours, for he shared in the recent exile of the
people, and returned with you. Well, Chaerephon, as
you know, was very impetuous in all his doings, and
5 he went to Delphi and boldly asked the oracle to tell
him whether—as I was saying, I must beg you not to
interrupt—he asked the oracle to tell him whether any
one was wiser than I was, and the Pythian prophetess
answered, that there was no man wiser. Chaerephon
10 is dead himself; but his brother, who is in court, will
confirm the truth of what I am saying.

*His efforts to interpret the oracle have earned him widespread
unpopularity in his search for true wisdom.*

B   Why do I mention this? Because I am going to
explain to you why I have such an evil name. When
I heard the answer, I said to myself, What can the
god mean? and what is the interpretation of his riddle?
5 for I know that I have no wisdom, small or great.
What then can he mean when he says that I am the
wisest of men? And yet he is a god, and cannot lie;
that would be against his nature. After long consideration, I thought of a method of trying the question.
C I reflected that if I could only find a man wiser than
myself, then I might go to the god with a refutation in
my hand. I should say to him, 'Here is a man who
is wiser than I am; but you said that I was the wisest.'
5 Accordingly I went to one who had the reputation of
wisdom, and observed him—his name I need not
mention; he was a politician whom I selected for
examination—and the result was as follows: When I
began to talk with him, I could not help thinking that
10 he was not really wise, although he was thought wise
by many, and still wiser by himself; and thereupon
I tried to explain to him that he thought himself wise,
D but was not really wise; and the consequence was
that he hated me, and his enmity was shared by several
who were present and heard me. So I left him,
saying to myself, as I went away: Well, although

I do not suppose that either of us knows anything 5
really beautiful and good, I am better off than he is
—for he knows nothing, and thinks that he knows;
I neither know nor think that I know. In this latter
particular, then, I seem to have slightly the advantage
of him. Then I went to another who had still higher 10
pretensions to wisdom, and my conclusion was exactly E
the same. Whereupon I made another enemy of him,
and of many others besides him.

*Having investigated the claims of the politicians to wisdom
without satisfaction, he examined the poets, who, though doubtless inspired, were certainly not wise.*

Μετὰ ταῦτ᾽ οὖν ἤδη ἐφεξῆς ᾖα, αἰσθανόμενος μὲν
[καὶ] λυπούμενος καὶ δεδιὼς ὅτι ἀπηχθανόμην, ὅμως δὲ 5
ἀναγκαῖον ἐδόκει εἶναι τὸ τοῦ θεοῦ περὶ πλείστου
ποιεῖσθαι· ἰτέον οὖν, σκοποῦντι τὸν χρησμὸν τί λέγει,
ἐπὶ ἅπαντας τούς τι δοκοῦντας εἰδέναι. καὶ νὴ τὸν
κύνα, ὦ ἄνδρες Ἀθηναῖοι—δεῖ γὰρ πρὸς ὑμᾶς τἀληθῆ 22
λέγειν—ἦ μὴν ἐγὼ ἔπαθόν τι τοιοῦτον· οἱ μὲν μάλιστα
εὐδοκιμοῦντες ἔδοξάν μοι ὀλίγου δεῖν τοῦ πλείστου
ἐνδεεῖς εἶναι ζητοῦντι κατὰ τὸν θεόν, ἄλλοι δὲ δοκοῦντες
φαυλότεροι ἐπιεικέστεροι εἶναι ἄνδρες πρὸς τὸ φρονίμως 5
ἔχειν. δεῖ δὴ ὑμῖν τὴν ἐμὴν πλάνην ἐπιδεῖξαι ὥσπερ
πόνους τινὰς πονοῦντος ἵνα μοι καὶ ἀνέλεγκτος ἡ
μαντεία γένοιτο. μετὰ γὰρ τοὺς πολιτικοὺς ᾖα ἐπὶ
τοὺς ποιητὰς τούς τε τῶν τραγῳδιῶν καὶ τοὺς τῶν
διθυράμβων καὶ τοὺς ἄλλους, ὡς ἐνταῦθα ἐπ᾽ αὐτοφώρῳ B
καταληψόμενος ἐμαυτὸν ἀμαθέστερον ἐκείνων ὄντα.
ἀναλαμβάνων οὖν αὐτῶν τὰ ποιήματα ἅ μοι ἐδόκει
μάλιστα πεπραγματεῦσθαι αὐτοῖς, διηρώτων ἂν αὐτοὺς
τί λέγοιεν, ἵν᾽ ἅμα τι καὶ μανθάνοιμι παρ᾽ αὐτῶν. 5
αἰσχύνομαι οὖν ὑμῖν εἰπεῖν, ὦ ἄνδρες, τἀληθῆ· ὅμως
δὲ ῥητέον. ὡς ἔπος γὰρ εἰπεῖν ὀλίγου αὐτῶν ἅπαντες
οἱ παρόντες ἂν βέλτιον ἔλεγον περὶ ὧν αὐτοὶ ἐπεποιή-
κεσαν. ἔγνων οὖν αὖ καὶ περὶ τῶν ποιητῶν ἐν ὀλίγῳ
τοῦτο, ὅτι οὐ σοφίᾳ ποιοῖεν ἃ ποιοῖεν, ἀλλὰ φύσει τινὶ C

καὶ ἐνθουσιάζοντες ὥσπερ οἱ θεομάντεις καὶ οἱ χρησμῳ-
δοί· καὶ γὰρ οὗτοι λέγουσι μὲν πολλὰ καὶ καλά, ἴσασιν
δὲ οὐδὲν ὧν λέγουσι. τοιοῦτόν τί μοι ἐφάνησαν πάθος
5 καὶ οἱ ποιηταὶ πεπονθότες, καὶ ἅμα ᾐσθόμην αὐτῶν
διὰ τὴν ποίησιν οἰομένων καὶ τἆλλα σοφωτάτων εἶναι
ἀνθρώπων ἃ οὐκ ἦσαν. ἀπῇα οὖν καὶ ἐντεῦθεν τῷ
αὐτῷ οἰόμενος περιγεγονέναι ᾧπερ καὶ τῶν πολιτικῶν.

The craftsmen too, wise in their own arts, wrongly held that
they were wise in other matters.

Τελευτῶν οὖν ἐπὶ τοὺς χειροτέχνας ᾖα· ἐμαυτῷ γὰρ
D συνῄδη οὐδὲν ἐπισταμένῳ ὡς ἔπος εἰπεῖν, τούτους δέ
γ᾽ ᾔδη ὅτι εὑρήσοιμι πολλὰ καὶ καλὰ ἐπισταμένους.
καὶ τούτου μὲν οὐκ ἐψεύσθην, ἀλλ᾽ ἠπίσταντο ἃ ἐγὼ
οὐκ ἠπιστάμην καί μου ταύτῃ σοφώτεροι ἦσαν. ἀλλ᾽,
5 ὦ ἄνδρες Ἀθηναῖοι, ταὐτόν μοι ἔδοξαν ἔχειν ἁμάρτημα
ὅπερ καὶ οἱ ποιηταὶ καὶ οἱ ἀγαθοὶ δημιουργοί—διὰ τὸ
τὴν τέχνην καλῶς ἐξεργάζεσθαι ἕκαστος ἠξίου καὶ
τἆλλα τὰ μέγιστα σοφώτατος εἶναι—καὶ αὐτῶν αὕτη
ἡ πλημμέλεια ἐκείνην τὴν σοφίαν ἀποκρύπτειν· ὥστε
E με ἐμαυτὸν ἀνερωτᾶν ὑπὲρ τοῦ χρησμοῦ πότερα δεξαίμην ἂν οὕτως ὥσπερ ἔχω ἔχειν, μήτε τι σοφὸς ὢν τὴν
ἐκείνων σοφίαν μήτε ἀμαθὴς τὴν ἀμαθίαν, ἢ ἀμφότερα
ἃ ἐκεῖνοι ἔχουσιν ἔχειν. ἀπεκρινάμην οὖν ἐμαυτῷ καὶ
5 τῷ χρησμῷ ὅτι μοι λυσιτελοῖ ὥσπερ ἔχω ἔχειν.

His conclusion as to the meaning of the oracle.

This inquisition has led to my having many enemies
23 of the worst and most dangerous kind, and has given
occasion also to many calumnies. And I am called
wise, for my hearers always imagine that I myself
possess the wisdom which I find wanting in others:
5 but the truth is, O men of Athens, that God only is
wise; and by his answer he intends to show that the
wisdom of men is worth little or nothing; he is not
speaking of Socrates, he is only using my name by way
B of illustration, as if he said, He, O men, is the wisest,
who, like Socrates, knows that his wisdom is in truth

worth nothing. And so I go about the world, obedient
to the god, and search and make inquiry into the wisdom
of any one, whether citizen or stranger, who appears to 5
be wise; and if he is not wise, then in vindication of
the oracle I show him that he is not wise; and my
occupation quite absorbs me, and I have no time to give
either to any public matter of interest or to any concern
of my own, but I am in utter poverty by reason of my C
devotion to the god.

*His methods of examination have been imitated by the young
men, the would-be wise exposed, and their indignation directed
against him.*

There is another thing :—young men of the richer
classes, who have not much to do, come about me of
their own accord : they like to hear the pretenders 5
examined, and they often imitate me, and proceed to
examine others ; there are plenty of persons, as they
quickly discover, who think that they know something,
but really know little or nothing ; and then those who
are examined by them instead of being angry with 10
themselves are angry with me : This confounded D
Socrates, they say ; this villainous misleader of youth !—
and then if somebody asks them, Why, what evil does
he practise or teach ? they do not know, and cannot
tell ; but in order that they may not appear to be at 5
a loss, they repeat the ready-made charges which are
used against all philosophers about teaching things up
in the clouds and under the earth, and having no gods,
and making the worse appear the better cause ; for they
do not like to confess that their pretence of knowledge 10
has been detected—which is the truth ; and as they
are numerous and ambitious and energetic, and are E
drawn up in battle array and have persuasive tongues,
they have filled your ears with their loud and inveterate
calumnies.

*This indignation has culminated in the charges brought by
Meletus, Anytus, and Lycon, who represent various interested
parties.*

'Εκ τούτων καὶ Μέλητός μοι ἐπέθετο καὶ Ἄνυτος καὶ 5
Λύκων, Μέλητος μὲν ὑπὲρ τῶν ποιητῶν ἀχθόμενος,

Ἄνυτος δὲ ὑπὲρ τῶν δημιουργῶν καὶ τῶν πολιτικῶν,
24 Λύκων δὲ ὑπὲρ τῶν ῥητόρων· ὥστε, ὅπερ ἀρχόμενος
ἐγὼ ἔλεγον, θαυμάζοιμ' ἂν εἰ οἷός τ' εἴην ἐγὼ ὑμῶν
ταύτην τὴν διαβολὴν ἐξελέσθαι ἐν οὕτως ὀλίγῳ χρόνῳ
οὕτω πολλὴν γεγονυῖαν. ταῦτ' ἔστιν ὑμῖν, ὦ ἄνδρες
5 Ἀθηναῖοι, τἀληθῆ, καὶ ὑμᾶς οὔτε μέγα οὔτε μικρὸν
ἀποκρυψάμενος ἐγὼ λέγω οὐδ' ὑποστειλάμενος. καίτοι
οἶδα σχεδὸν ὅτι αὐτοῖς τούτοις ἀπεχθάνομαι, ὃ καὶ
τεκμήριον ὅτι ἀληθῆ λέγω καὶ ὅτι αὕτη ἐστὶν ἡ δια-
B βολὴ ἡ ἐμὴ καὶ τὰ αἴτια ταῦτά ἐστιν. καὶ ἐάντε νῦν
ἐάντε αὖθις ζητήσητε ταῦτα, οὕτως εὑρήσετε.

*He proceeds to deal with the specific charges contained in the
indictment.*

Περὶ μὲν οὖν ὧν οἱ πρῶτοί μου κατήγοροι κατηγόρουν
αὕτη ἔστω ἱκανὴ ἀπολογία πρὸς ὑμᾶς· πρὸς δὲ Μέλητον
5 τὸν ἀγαθὸν καὶ φιλόπολιν, ὥς φησι, καὶ τοὺς ὑστέρους
μετὰ ταῦτα πειράσομαι ἀπολογήσασθαι. αὖθις γὰρ δή,
ὥσπερ ἑτέρων τούτων ὄντων κατηγόρων, λάβωμεν αὖ
τὴν τούτων ἀντωμοσίαν. ἔχει δέ πως ὧδε· Σωκράτη
φησὶν ἀδικεῖν τούς τε νέους διαφθείροντα καὶ θεοὺς οὓς
c ἡ πόλις νομίζει οὐ νομίζοντα, ἕτερα δὲ δαιμόνια καινά.
τὸ μὲν δὴ ἔγκλημα τοιοῦτόν ἐστιν· τούτου δὲ τοῦ ἐγκλή-
ματος ἓν ἕκαστον ἐξετάσωμεν.

Φησὶ γὰρ δὴ τοὺς νέους ἀδικεῖν με διαφθείροντα.
5 ἐγὼ δέ γε, ὦ ἄνδρες Ἀθηναῖοι, ἀδικεῖν φημι Μέλητον,
ὅτι σπουδῇ χαριεντίζεται, ῥᾳδίως εἰς ἀγῶνα καθιστὰς
ἀνθρώπους, περὶ πραγμάτων προσποιούμενος σπουδάζειν
καὶ κήδεσθαι ὧν οὐδὲν τούτῳ πώποτε ἐμέλησεν· ὡς δὲ
τοῦτο οὕτως ἔχει, πειράσομαι καὶ ὑμῖν ἐπιδεῖξαι.

*Meletus in cross-examination attempts to maintain that
Socrates alone corrupts the young men.*

10 Come hither, Meletus, and let me ask a question
of you. You think a great deal about the improvement
of youth?
Yes, I do.

Tell the judges, then, who is their improver; for D
you must know, as you have taken the pains to discover their corrupter, and are citing and accusing me
before them. Speak, then, and tell the judges who
their improver is.—Observe, Meletus, that you are 5
silent, and have nothing to say. But is not this rather
disgraceful, and a very considerable proof of what I
was saying, that you have no interest in the matter?
Speak up, friend, and tell us who their improver is.

The laws.   10

But that, my good sir, is not my meaning. I want to E
know who the person is, who, in the first place, knows
the laws.

The judges, Socrates, who are present in court.

What, do you mean to say, Meletus, that they are 5
able to instruct and improve youth?

Certainly they are.

What, all of them, or some only and not others?

All of them.

By the goddess Hera, that is good news! There are 10
plenty of improvers, then. And what do you say of the
audience,—do they improve them?   **25**

Yes, they do.

And the senators?

Yes, the senators improve them.

But perhaps the members of the assembly corrupt 5
them?—or do they improve them?

They improve them.

Then every Athenian improves and elevates them;
all with the exception of myself; and I alone am their
corrupter? Is that what you affirm?   10

That is what I stoutly affirm.

I am very unfortunate if you are right. But suppose
I ask you a question: How about horses? Does one
man do them harm and all the world good? Is not B
the exact opposite the truth? One man is able to do
them good, or at least not many—the trainer of horses,
that is to say, does them good, and others who have to
do with them rather injure them? Is not that true, 5
Meletus, of horses, or of any other animals? Most
assuredly it is; whether you and Anytus say yes or
no. Happy indeed would be the condition of youth

if they had one corrupter only, and all the rest of
c the world were their improvers. But you, Meletus,
have sufficiently shown that you never had a thought
about the young: your carelessness is seen in your
not caring about the very things which you bring
5 against me.

*The cross-examination of Meletus continued. Does he main-
tain that Socrates is voluntarily doing himself deliberate harm?*

And now, Meletus, I will ask you another question
—by Zeus I will: Which is better, to live among bad
citizens, or among good ones? Answer, friend, I say;
the question is one which may be easily answered. Do
10 not the good do their neighbours good, and the bad do
them evil?

Certainly.

And is there any one who would rather be injured
D than benefited by those who live with him? Answer,
my good friend, the law requires you to answer—does
any one like to be injured?

Certainly not.

5 And when you accuse me of corrupting and deterio-
rating the youth, do you allege that I corrupt them
intentionally or unintentionally?

Intentionally, I say.

But you have just admitted that the good do their
10 neighbours good, and the evil do them evil. Now, is
E that a truth which your superior wisdom has recognized
thus early in life, and am I, at my age, in such darkness
and ignorance as not to know that if a man with whom
I have to live is corrupted by me, I am very likely to
5 be harmed by him; and yet I corrupt him, and intentionally, too—so you say, although neither I nor any
other human being is ever likely to be convinced by
you. But either I do not corrupt them, or I corrupt
them unintentionally; and on either view of the case
26 you lie. If my offence is unintentional, the law has no
cognizance of unintentional offences: you ought to have
taken me privately, and warned and admonished me,
for if I had been better advised, I should have left
5 off doing what I only did unintentionally—no doubt
I should; but you would have nothing to say to me

and refused to teach me. And now you bring me up in this court, which is a place not of instruction, but of punishment.

Meletus has falsely attributed the scientific doctrines of Anaxagoras to Socrates, and is involved in a contradiction when he calls him an atheist.

Ἀλλὰ γάρ, ὦ ἄνδρες Ἀθηναῖοι, τοῦτο μὲν ἤδη δῆλον 10 οὑγὼ ἔλεγον, ὅτι Μελήτῳ τούτων οὔτε μέγα οὔτε μικρὸν B πώποτε ἐμέλησεν. ὅμως δὲ δὴ λέγε ἡμῖν, πῶς με φῇς διαφθείρειν, ὦ Μέλητε, τοὺς νεωτέρους; ἢ δῆλον δὴ ὅτι κατὰ τὴν γραφὴν ἣν ἐγράψω θεοὺς διδάσκοντα μὴ νομίζειν οὓς ἡ πόλις νομίζει, ἕτερα δὲ δαιμόνια καινά; 5 οὐ ταῦτα λέγεις ὅτι διδάσκων διαφθείρω;

Πάνυ μὲν οὖν σφόδρα ταῦτα λέγω.

Πρὸς αὐτῶν τοίνυν, ὦ Μέλητε, τούτων τῶν θεῶν ὧν νῦν ὁ λόγος ἐστίν, εἰπὲ ἔτι σαφέστερον καὶ ἐμοὶ καὶ τοῖς ἀνδράσιν τουτοισί. ἐγὼ γὰρ οὐ δύναμαι μαθεῖν C πότερον λέγεις διδάσκειν με νομίζειν εἶναί τινας θεούς —καὶ αὐτὸς ἄρα νομίζω εἶναι θεοὺς καὶ οὐκ εἰμὶ τὸ παράπαν ἄθεος οὐδὲ ταύτῃ ἀδικῶ—οὐ μέντοι οὕσπερ γε ἡ πόλις ἀλλὰ ἑτέρους, καὶ τοῦτ' ἔστιν ὅ μοι ἐγκαλεῖς, 5 ὅτι ἑτέρους, ἢ παντάπασί με φῇς οὔτε αὐτὸν νομίζειν θεοὺς τούς τε ἄλλους ταῦτα διδάσκειν.

Ταῦτα λέγω, ὡς τὸ παράπαν οὐ νομίζεις θεούς.

Ὦ θαυμάσιε Μέλητε, ἵνα τί ταῦτα λέγεις; οὐδὲ D ἥλιον οὐδὲ σελήνην ἄρα νομίζω θεοὺς εἶναι, ὥσπερ οἱ ἄλλοι ἄνθρωποι;

Μὰ Δί', ὦ ἄνδρες δικασταί, ἐπεὶ τὸν μὲν ἥλιον λίθον φησὶν εἶναι, τὴν δὲ σελήνην γῆν. 5

Ἀναξαγόρου οἴει κατηγορεῖν, ὦ φίλε Μέλητε; καὶ οὕτω καταφρονεῖς τῶνδε καὶ οἴει αὐτοὺς ἀπείρους γραμμάτων εἶναι ὥστε οὐκ εἰδέναι ὅτι τὰ Ἀναξαγόρου βιβλία τοῦ Κλαζομενίου γέμει τούτων τῶν λόγων; καὶ δὴ καὶ οἱ νέοι ταῦτα παρ' ἐμοῦ μανθάνουσιν, ἃ ἔξεστιν ἐνίοτε 10

E εἰ πάνυ πολλοῦ δραχμῆς ἐκ τῆς ὀρχήστρας πριαμένοις
Σωκράτους καταγελᾶν, ἐὰν προσποιῆται ἑαυτοῦ εἶναι,
ἄλλως τε καὶ οὕτως ἄτοπα ὄντα; ἀλλ', ὦ πρὸς Διός,
οὑτωσί σοι δοκῶ; οὐδένα νομίζω θεὸν εἶναι;
5   Οὐ μέντοι μὰ Δία οὐδ' ὁπωστιοῦν.
      Ἄπιστός γ' εἶ, ὦ Μέλητε, καὶ ταῦτα μέντοι, ὡς ἐμοὶ
δοκεῖς, σαυτῷ. ἐμοὶ γὰρ δοκεῖ οὑτοσί, ὦ ἄνδρες
Ἀθηναῖοι, πάνυ εἶναι ὑβριστὴς καὶ ἀκόλαστος, καὶ
ἀτεχνῶς τὴν γραφὴν ταύτην ὕβρει τινὶ καὶ ἀκολασίᾳ
10 καὶ νεότητι γράψασθαι. ἔοικεν γὰρ ὥσπερ αἴνιγμα
27 συντιθέντι διαπειρωμένῳ "Ἆρα γνώσεται Σωκράτης
ὁ σοφὸς δὴ ἐμοῦ χαριεντιζομένου καὶ ἐναντί' ἐμαυτῷ
λέγοντος, ἢ ἐξαπατήσω αὐτὸν καὶ τοὺς ἄλλους τοὺς
ἀκούοντας;" οὗτος γὰρ ἐμοὶ φαίνεται τὰ ἐναντία λέγειν
5 αὐτὸς ἑαυτῷ ἐν τῇ γραφῇ ὥσπερ ἂν εἰ εἴποι· "Ἀδικεῖ
Σωκράτης θεοὺς οὐ νομίζων, ἀλλὰ θεοὺς νομίζων."
καίτοι τοῦτό ἐστι παίζοντος.

*The contradiction demonstrated. Socrates attaches little im-
portance to his present accusers by comparison with the old
prejudices.*

I should like you, O men of Athens, to join me in
examining what I conceive to be his inconsistency ; and
10 do you, Meletus, answer. And I must remind the
B audience of my request that they would not make
a disturbance if I speak in my accustomed manner :
      Did ever man, Meletus, believe in the existence of
human things, and not of human beings ? . . . 1 wish,
5 men of Athens, that he would answer, and not be
always trying to get up an interruption. Did ever any
man believe in horsemanship, and not in horses ? or in
flute-playing, and not in flute-players ? No. my friend ;
I will answer to you and to the court, as you refuse to
10 answer for yourself. There is no man who ever did.
But now please to answer the next question : Can a man
C believe in spiritual and divine agencies, and not in spirits
or demigods ?
He cannot.

How lucky I am to have extracted that answer, by the assistance of the court! But then you swear in the 5 indictment that I teach and believe in divine or spiritual agencies (new or old, no matter for that); at any rate, I believe in spiritual agencies—so you say and swear in the affidavit—and yet if I believe in divine beings, how can I help believing in spirits or demigods, must I 10 not? To be sure I must; and therefore I may assume that your silence gives consent. Now what are spirits or demigods? are they not either gods or the sons of gods? D
Certainly they are.

But this is what I call the facetious riddle invented by you: the demigods or spirits are gods, and you say first that I do not believe in gods, and then again that 5 I do believe in gods; that is, if I believe in demigods. For if the demigods are the illegitimate sons of gods, whether by the nymphs or by any other mothers, of whom they are said to be the sons—what human being will ever believe that there are no gods if they are the 10 sons of gods? You might as well affirm the existence of mules, and deny that of horses and asses. Such E nonsense, Meletus, could only have been intended by you to make trial of me. You have put this into the indictment because you had nothing real of which to accuse me. But no one who has a particle of under- 5 standing will ever be convinced by you that the same men can believe in divine and superhuman things, and yet not believe that there are gods and demigods and heroes. 28

I have said enough in answer to the charge of Meletus: any elaborate defence is unnecessary; but I know only too well how many are the enmities which I have incurred, and this is what will be my destruction 5 if I am destroyed—not Meletus, nor yet Anytus, but the envy and detraction of the world, which has been the death of many good men, and will probably be the death of many more; there is no danger of my being B the last of them.

His decision to do right at all costs has brought him into a dangerous position, but he cannot save his life at the cost of sacrificing his conscience.

Some one will say: And are you not ashamed,

Socrates, of a course of life which is likely to bring you to an untimely end? To him I may fairly answer: There you are mistaken: a man who is good for anything ought not to calculate the chance of living or dying; he ought only to consider whether in doing anything he is doing right or wrong—acting the part of a good man or of a bad. Whereas, upon your view, the heroes who fell at Troy were not good for much, and the son of Thetis above all, who altogether despised danger in comparison with disgrace; and when he was so eager to slay Hector, his goddess mother said to him, that if he avenged his companion Patroclus, and slew Hector, he would die himself—'Fate', she said, in these or the like words, 'waits for you next after Hector;' he, receiving this warning, utterly despised danger and death, and instead of fearing them, feared rather to live in dishonour, and not to avenge his friend. 'Let me die forthwith,' he replies, 'and be avenged of my enemy, rather than abide here by the beaked ships, a laughing-stock and a burden of the earth.' Had Achilles any thought of death and danger?

He can only remain at his post in obedience to the orders of God, as he did on active service in obedience to earthly commanders. Death may not be an evil, disgrace certainly is.

Οὕτω γὰρ ἔχει, ὦ ἄνδρες Ἀθηναῖοι, τῇ ἀληθείᾳ· οὗ ἄν τις ἑαυτὸν τάξῃ ἡγησάμενος βέλτιστον εἶναι ἢ ὑπ' ἄρχοντος ταχθῇ, ἐνταῦθα δεῖ, ὡς ἐμοὶ δοκεῖ, μένοντα κινδυνεύειν, μηδὲν ὑπολογιζόμενον μήτε θάνατον μήτε ἄλλο μηδὲν πρὸ τοῦ αἰσχροῦ. ἐγὼ οὖν δεινὰ ἂν εἴην εἰργασμένος, ὦ ἄνδρες Ἀθηναῖοι, εἰ ὅτε μέν με οἱ ἄρχοντες ἔταττον, οὓς ὑμεῖς εἵλεσθε ἄρχειν μου, καὶ ἐν Ποτειδαίᾳ καὶ ἐν Ἀμφιπόλει καὶ ἐπὶ Δηλίῳ, τότε μὲν οὖ ἐκεῖνοι ἔταττον ἔμενον ὥσπερ καὶ ἄλλος τις καὶ ἐκινδύνευον ἀποθανεῖν, τοῦ δὲ θεοῦ τάττοντος, ὡς ἐγὼ ᾠήθην τε καὶ ὑπέλαβον, φιλοσοφοῦντά με δεῖν ζῆν καὶ ἐξετάζοντα ἐμαυτὸν καὶ τοὺς ἄλλους, ἐνταῦθα δὲ φοβηθεὶς ἢ θάνατον ἢ ἄλλ' ὁτιοῦν πρᾶγμα λίποιμι τὴν τάξιν. δεινόν τἂν εἴη, καὶ ὡς ἀληθῶς τότ' ἄν με

δικαίως εἰσάγοι τις εἰς δικαστήριον, ὅτι οὐ νομίζω 29
θεοὺς εἶναι ἀπειθῶν τῇ μαντείᾳ καὶ δεδιὼς θάνατον καὶ
οἰόμενος σοφὸς εἶναι οὐκ ὤν. τὸ γάρ τοι θάνατον
δεδιέναι, ὦ ἄνδρες, οὐδὲν ἄλλο ἐστὶν ἢ δοκεῖν σοφὸν
εἶναι μὴ ὄντα· δοκεῖν γὰρ εἰδέναι ἐστὶν ἃ οὐκ οἶδεν. 5
οἶδε μὲν γὰρ οὐδεὶς τὸν θάνατον οὐδ᾽ εἰ τυγχάνει τῷ
ἀνθρώπῳ πάντων μέγιστον ὂν τῶν ἀγαθῶν, δεδίασι
δ᾽ ὡς εὖ εἰδότες ὅτι μέγιστον τῶν κακῶν ἐστι. καίτοι B
πῶς οὐκ ἀμαθία ἐστὶν αὕτη ἡ ἐπονείδιστος, ἡ τοῦ
οἴεσθαι εἰδέναι ἃ οὐκ οἶδεν; ἐγὼ δ᾽, ὦ ἄνδρες, τούτῳ
καὶ ἐνταῦθα ἴσως διαφέρω τῶν πολλῶν ἀνθρώπων, καὶ
εἰ δή τῳ σοφώτερός του φαίην εἶναι, τούτῳ ἄν, ὅτι οὐκ 5
εἰδὼς ἱκανῶς περὶ τῶν ἐν Ἅιδου οὕτω καὶ οἴομαι οὐκ
εἰδέναι· τὸ δὲ ἀδικεῖν καὶ ἀπειθεῖν τῷ βελτίονι καὶ θεῷ
καὶ ἀνθρώπῳ, ὅτι κακὸν καὶ αἰσχρόν ἐστιν οἶδα. πρὸ
οὖν τῶν κακῶν ὧν οἶδα ὅτι κακά ἐστιν, ἃ μὴ οἶδα εἰ
καὶ ἀγαθὰ ὄντα τυγχάνει οὐδέποτε φοβήσομαι οὐδὲ 10
φεύξομαι.

*He cannot give up his mission. He has been appointed by
God to convince his fellow-men of ignorance and of the need for
caring for the soul above all things.*

And therefore if you let me go now, and are not convinced by Anytus, who said that since I had been c
prosecuted I must be put to death (or if not that I
ought never to have been prosecuted at all); and that if
I escape now, your sons will all be utterly ruined by
listening to my words—if you say to me, Socrates, this 5
time we will not mind Anytus, and you shall be let off,
but upon one condition, that you are not to inquire and
speculate in this way any more, and that if you are
caught doing so again you shall die—if this was the D
condition on which you let me go, I should reply:
Men of Athens, I honour and love you; but I shall
obey God rather than you, and while I have life and
strength I shall never cease from the practice and 5
teaching of philosophy, exhorting any one whom I meet
and saying to him after my manner: You, my friend,

—a citizen of the great and mighty and wise city of Athens—are you not ashamed of heaping up the greatest
E amount of money and honour and reputation, and caring so little about wisdom and truth and the greatest improvement of the soul, which you never regard or heed at all ?   And if the person with whom I am arguing,
5 says : Yes, but I do care ; then I do not leave him or let him go at once ; but I proceed to interrogate and examine and cross-examine him, and if I think that he has no virtue in him, but only says that he has,
30 I reproach him with undervaluing the greater, and overvaluing the less.   And I shall repeat the same words to every one whom I meet, young and old, citizen and alien, but especially to the citizens inasmuch
5 as they are my brethren.   For know that this is the command of God ; and I believe that no greater good has ever happened in the state than my service to the God.   For I do nothing but go about persuading you all, old and young alike, not to take thought for your
B persons or your properties, but first and chiefly to care about the greatest improvement of the soul.   I tell you that virtue is not given by money, but that from virtue comes money and every other good of man, public as
5 well as private.   This is my teaching, and if this is the doctrine which corrupts the youth, I am a mischievous person.   But if any one says that this is not my teaching, he is speaking an untruth.   Wherefore, O men of Athens, I say to you, do as Anytus bids or not as
10 Anytus bids, and either acquit me or not ; but whichever you do, understand that I shall never alter my
c ways, not even if I have to die many times.

If the Athenians kill him, they will harm themselves rather than him ; they will not easily find another man to goad them out of their sleep of ignorance and self-satisfaction.

Μὴ θορυβεῖτε, ὦ ἄνδρες Ἀθηναῖοι, ἀλλ᾽ ἐμμείνατέ μοι οἷς ἐδεήθην ὑμῶν, μὴ θορυβεῖν ἐφ᾽ οἷς ἂν λέγω ἀλλ᾽ ἀκούειν· καὶ γάρ, ὡς ἐγὼ οἶμαι, ὀνήσεσθε ἀκούοντες.
5 μέλλω γὰρ οὖν ἄττα ὑμῖν ἐρεῖν καὶ ἄλλα ἐφ᾽ οἷς ἴσως βοήσεσθε· ἀλλὰ μηδαμῶς ποιεῖτε τοῦτο. εὖ γὰρ ἴστε, ἐάν με ἀποκτείνητε τοιοῦτον ὄντα οἷον ἐγὼ λέγω, οὐκ

SCENE I. THE TRIAL 39

ἂν βλάψειεν οὔτε Μέλητος οὔτε Ἄνυτος—οὐδὲ γὰρ ἂν
δύναιτο—οὐ γὰρ οἴομαι θεμιτὸν εἶναι ἀμείνονι ἀνδρὶ D
ὑπὸ χείρονος βλάπτεσθαι. ἀποκτείνειε μεντἂν ἴσως
ἢ ἐξελάσειεν ἢ ἀτιμώσειεν· ἀλλὰ ταῦτα οὗτος μὲν
ἴσως οἴεται καὶ ἄλλος τίς που μεγάλα κακά, ἐγὼ δ᾽ οὐκ
οἴομαι, ἀλλὰ πολὺ μᾶλλον ποιεῖν ἃ οὑτοσὶ νῦν ποιεῖ, 5
ἄνδρα ἀδίκως ἐπιχειρεῖν ἀποκτεινύναι. νῦν οὖν, ὦ
ἄνδρες Ἀθηναῖοι, πολλοῦ δέω ἐγὼ ὑπὲρ ἐμαυτοῦ ἀπο-
λογεῖσθαι, ὥς τις ἂν οἴοιτο, ἀλλὰ ὑπὲρ ὑμῶν, μή τι
ἐξαμάρτητε περὶ τὴν τοῦ θεοῦ δόσιν ὑμῖν ἐμοῦ καταψηφισάμενοι. ἐὰν γάρ με ἀποκτείνητε, οὐ ῥᾳδίως E
ἄλλον τοιοῦτον εὑρήσετε, ἀτεχνῶς—εἰ καὶ γελοιότερον
εἰπεῖν—προσκείμενον τῇ πόλει ὑπὸ τοῦ θεοῦ ὥσπερ
ἵππῳ μεγάλῳ μὲν καὶ γενναίῳ, ὑπὸ μεγέθους δὲ νωθε-
στέρῳ καὶ δεομένῳ ἐγείρεσθαι ὑπὸ μύωπός τινος, οἷον δή 5
μοι δοκεῖ ὁ θεὸς ἐμὲ τῇ πόλει προστεθηκέναι τοιοῦτόν
τινα, ὃς ὑμᾶς ἐγείρων καὶ πείθων καὶ ὀνειδίζων ἕνα
ἕκαστον οὐδὲν παύομαι τὴν ἡμέραν ὅλην πανταχοῦ
προσκαθίζων. τοιοῦτος οὖν ἄλλος οὐ ῥᾳδίως ὑμῖν 31
γενήσεται, ὦ ἄνδρες, ἀλλ᾽ ἐὰν ἐμοὶ πείθησθε, φείσεσθέ
μου· ὑμεῖς δ᾽ ἴσως τάχ᾽ ἂν ἀχθόμενοι, ὥσπερ οἱ νυστά-
ζοντες ἐγειρόμενοι, κρούσαντες ἄν με, πειθόμενοι Ἀνύτῳ,
ῥᾳδίως ἂν ἀποκτείναιτε, εἶτα τὸν λοιπὸν βίον καθεύ- 5
δοντες διατελοῖτε ἄν, εἰ μή τινα ἄλλον ὁ θεὸς ὑμῖν
ἐπιπέμψειεν κηδόμενος ὑμῶν.

*His poverty witnesses the earnestness with which he has given
up all in order to pursue his divinely appointed mission.*

When I say that I am given to you by God, the **B**
proof of my mission is this:—if I had been like other
men, I should not have neglected all my own concerns
or patiently seen the neglect of them during all these
years, and have been doing yours, coming to you in- **5**
dividually like a father or elder brother, exhorting you
to regard virtue ; such conduct, I say, would be unlike

human nature. If I had gained anything, or if my ex-
hortations had been paid, there would have been some
10 sense in my doing so ; but now, as you will perceive,
c not even the impudence of my accusers dares to say
that I have ever exacted or sought pay of any one ; of
that they have no witness. And I have a sufficient
witness to the truth of what I say—my poverty.

*He describes the ' divine sign ', which has prevented him from
engaging in politics, an occupation in which no honest man
could survive for long.*

5 Some one may wonder why I go about in private
giving advice and busying myself with the concerns of
others, but do not venture to come forward in public
and advise the state. I will tell you why. You have
heard me speak at sundry times and in divers places of
d an oracle or sign which comes to me, and is the divinity
which Meletus ridicules in the indictment. This sign,
which is a kind of voice, first began to come to me when
I was a child ; it always forbids but never commands
5 me to do anything which I am going to do. This is
what deters me from being a politician. And rightly,
as I think. For I am certain, O men of Athens, that
if I had engaged in politics, I should have perished long
E ago, and done no good either to you or to myself.
And do not be offended at my telling you the truth :
for the truth is, that no man who goes to war with you
or any other multitude, honestly striving against the
5 many lawless and unrighteous deeds which are done in
32 a state, will save his life ; he who will fight for the
right, if he would live even for a brief space, must have
a private station and not a public one.

*He recalls two occasions on which in a public capacity he all
but sacrificed his life in maintaining the right, once under the
democracy, and once under the Thirty Tyrants.*

Μεγάλα δ' ἔγωγε ὑμῖν τεκμήρια παρέξομαι τούτων,
5 οὐ λόγους ἀλλ' ἃ ὑμεῖς τιμᾶτε, ἔργα. ἀκούσατε δή μοι
τὰ συμβεβηκότα, ἵνα εἰδῆτε ὅτι οὐδ' ἂν ἑνὶ ὑπεικάθοιμι
παρὰ τὸ δίκαιον δείσας θάνατον, μὴ ὑπείκων δὲ ἀλλὰ
κἂν ἀπολοίμην. ἐρῶ δὲ ὑμῖν φορτικὰ μὲν καὶ δικανικά.

ἀληθῆ δέ. ἐγὼ γάρ, ὦ ἄνδρες Ἀθηναῖοι, ἄλλην μὲν
ἀρχὴν οὐδεμίαν πώποτε ἦρξα ἐν τῇ πόλει, ἐβούλευσα B
δέ· καὶ ἔτυχεν ἡμῶν ἡ φυλὴ [Ἀντιοχὶς] πρυτανεύουσα
ὅτε ὑμεῖς τοὺς δέκα στρατηγοὺς τοὺς οὐκ ἀνελομένους
τοὺς ἐκ τῆς ναυμαχίας ἐβουλεύσασθε ἀθρόους κρίνειν,
παρανόμως, ὡς ἐν τῷ ὑστέρῳ χρόνῳ πᾶσιν ὑμῖν ἔδοξεν. 5
τότ' ἐγὼ μόνος τῶν πρυτάνεων ἠναντιώθην ὑμῖν μηδὲν
ποιεῖν παρὰ τοὺς νόμους καὶ ἐναντία ἐψηφισάμην· καὶ
ἑτοίμων ὄντων ἐνδεικνύναι με καὶ ἀπάγειν τῶν ῥητόρων,
καὶ ὑμῶν κελευόντων καὶ βοώντων, μετὰ τοῦ νόμου καὶ
τοῦ δικαίου ᾤμην μᾶλλόν με δεῖν διακινδυνεύειν ἢ μεθ' C
ὑμῶν γενέσθαι μὴ δίκαια βουλευομένων, φοβηθέντα
δεσμὸν ἢ θάνατον. καὶ ταῦτα μὲν ἦν ἔτι δημοκρατου-
μένης τῆς πόλεως· ἐπειδὴ δὲ ὀλιγαρχία ἐγένετο, οἱ
τριάκοντα αὖ μεταπεμψάμενοί με πέμπτον αὐτὸν εἰς 5
τὴν θόλον προσέταξαν ἀγαγεῖν ἐκ Σαλαμῖνος Λέοντα
τὸν Σαλαμίνιον ἵνα ἀποθάνοι, οἷα δὴ καὶ ἄλλοις ἐκεῖνοι
πολλοῖς πολλὰ προσέταττον, βουλόμενοι ὡς πλείστους
ἀναπλῆσαι αἰτιῶν. τότε μέντοι ἐγὼ οὐ λόγῳ ἀλλ' ἔργῳ D
αὖ ἐνεδειξάμην ὅτι ἐμοὶ θανάτου μὲν μέλει, εἰ μὴ
ἀγροικότερον ἦν εἰπεῖν, οὐδ' ὁτιοῦν, τοῦ δὲ μηδὲν ἄδικον
μηδ' ἀνόσιον ἐργάζεσθαι, τούτου δὲ τὸ πᾶν μέλει. ἐμὲ
γὰρ ἐκείνη ἡ ἀρχὴ οὐκ ἐξέπληξεν, οὕτως ἰσχυρὰ οὖσα, 5
ὥστε ἄδικόν τι ἐργάσασθαι, ἀλλ' ἐπειδὴ ἐκ τῆς θόλου
ἐξήλθομεν, οἱ μὲν τέτταρες ᾤχοντο εἰς Σαλαμῖνα καὶ
ἤγαγον Λέοντα, ἐγὼ δὲ ᾠχόμην ἀπιὼν οἴκαδε. καὶ
ἴσως ἂν διὰ ταῦτα ἀπέθανον, εἰ μὴ ἡ ἀρχὴ διὰ ταχέων
κατελύθη. καὶ τούτων ὑμῖν ἔσονται πολλοὶ μάρτυρες. E

*In spite of all that is said to the contrary, he is neither
politician nor teacher.*

Now do you really imagine that I could have survived
all these years, if I had led a public life, supposing
that like a good man I had always maintained the right
and had made justice, as I ought, the first thing? No 5
indeed, men of Athens, neither I nor any other man.

33 But I have always been the same in all my actions,
public as well as private, and never have I yielded any
base compliance to those who are slanderously termed
my disciples, or to any other. Not that I have any
5 regular disciples. But if any one likes to come and
hear me while I am pursuing my mission, whether he
be young or old, he is not excluded. Nor do I converse only with those who pay ; but any one, whether
B he be rich or poor, may ask and answer me and listen
to my words ; and whether he turns out to be a bad
man or a good one, neither result can be justly imputed
to me ; for I never taught or professed to teach him
5 anything. And if any one says that he has ever learned
or heard anything from me in private which all the world
has not heard, let me tell you that he is lying.

*If he has corrupted the young men, how is it that neither they
nor any of their relatives have come forward to give evidence
against him?*

But I shall be asked, Why do people delight in con-
c tinually conversing with you ? I have told you already,
Athenians, the whole truth about this matter : they
like to hear the cross-examination of the pretenders
to wisdom ; there is amusement in it. Now this duty
5 of cross-examining other men has been imposed upon
me by God ; and has been signified to me by oracles,
visions, and in every way in which the will of divine
power was ever intimated to any one. This is true, O
Athenians ; or, if not true, would be soon refuted.
D If I am or have been corrupting the youth, those of
them who are now grown up and have become sensible
that I gave them bad advice in the days of their youth
should come forward as accusers, and take their re-
5 venge ; or if they do not like to come themselves, some
of their relatives, fathers, brothers, or other kinsmen,
should say what evil their families have suffered at my
hands. Now is their time. Many of them I see in the
court. There is Crito, who is of the same age and of
10 the same deme with myself, and there is Critobulus his
son, whom I also see. Then again there is Lysanias
of Sphettus, who is the father of Aeschines—he is
E present ; and also there is Antiphon of Cephisus, who

is the father of Epigenes ; and there are the brothers
of several who have associated with me. There is
Nicostratus the son of Theozotides, and the brother
of Theodotus (now Theodotus himself is dead, and 5
therefore he, at any rate, will not seek to stop him) ;
and there is Paralus the son of Demodocus, who had
a brother Theages ; and Adeimantus the son of Ariston, 34
whose brother Plato is present ; and Aeantodorus, who
is the brother of Apollodorus, whom I also see. I might
mention a great many others, some of whom Meletus
should have produced as witnesses in the course of his 5
speech ; and let him still produce them, if he has for-
gotten—I will make way for him. And let him say if
he has any testimony of the sort which he can produce.
Nay, Athenians, the very opposite is the truth. For all
these are ready to witness on behalf of the corrupter, of 10
the injurer of their kindred, as Meletus and Anytus B
call me ; not the corrupted youth only—there might
have been a motive for that—but their uncorrupted elder
relatives. Why should they too support me with their
testimony ? Why, indeed, except for the sake of truth 5
and justice, and because they know that I am speaking
the truth, and that Meletus is a liar.

*In justice to himself he can make none of the customary
appeals to the emotions of the jury.*

Well, Athenians, this and the like of this is all the
defence which I have to offer. Yet a word more.
Perhaps there may be some one who is offended at me, 10
when he calls to mind how he himself on a similar, c
or even a less serious occasion, prayed and entreated
the judges with many tears, and how he produced his
children in court, which was a moving spectacle, together with a host of relations and friends ; whereas 5
I, who am probably in danger of my life, will do none
of these things. The contrast may occur to his mind,
and he may be set against me, and vote in anger because he is displeased at me on this account. Now if
there be such a person among you—mind, I do not D
say that there is—to him I may fairly reply : My
friend, I am a man, and like other men, a creature of
flesh and blood, and not 'of wood or stone', as Homer

5 says; and I have a family, yes, and sons, O Athenians,
three in number, one almost a man, and two others
who are still young; and yet I will not bring any of
them hither in order to petition you for an acquittal.
And why not? Not from any self-assertion or want
E of respect for you. Whether I am or am not afraid of
death is another question, of which I will not now
speak. But, having regard to public opinion, I feel
that such conduct would be discreditable to myself, and
5 to you, and to the whole state. One who has reached
my years, and who has a name for wisdom, ought not
to demean himself. Whether this opinion of me be
deserved or not, at any rate the world has decided that
35 Socrates is in some way superior to other men.

*It is wrong to try to move a jury to compassion by these
means, for it is an incitement to them to grant favours instead
of doing justice according to their oath.*

Εἰ οὖν ὑμῶν οἱ δοκοῦντες διαφέρειν εἴτε σοφίᾳ εἴτε
ἀνδρείᾳ εἴτε ἄλλῃ ἡτινιοῦν ἀρετῇ τοιοῦτοι ἔσονται,
αἰσχρὸν ἂν εἴη· οἵουσπερ ἐγὼ πολλάκις ἑώρακά τινας
5 ὅταν κρίνωνται, δοκοῦντας μέν τι εἶναι, θαυμάσια δὲ
ἐργαζομένους, ὡς δεινόν τι οἰομένους πείσεσθαι εἰ ἀπο-
θανοῦνται, ὥσπερ ἀθανάτων ἐσομένων ἂν ὑμεῖς αὐτοὺς
μὴ ἀποκτείνητε· οἳ ἐμοὶ δοκοῦσιν αἰσχύνην τῇ πόλει
B περιάπτειν, ὥστ᾽ ἄν τινα καὶ τῶν ξένων ὑπολαβεῖν ὅτι
οἱ διαφέροντες Ἀθηναίων εἰς ἀρετήν, οὓς αὐτοὶ ἑαυτῶν
ἔν τε ταῖς ἀρχαῖς καὶ ταῖς ἄλλαις τιμαῖς προκρίνουσιν,
οὗτοι γυναικῶν οὐδὲν διαφέρουσιν. ταῦτα γάρ, ὦ ἄνδρες
5 Ἀθηναῖοι, οὔτε ὑμᾶς χρὴ ποιεῖν τοὺς δοκοῦντας καὶ
ὁπηοῦν τι εἶναι, οὔτ᾽, ἂν ἡμεῖς ποιῶμεν, ὑμᾶς ἐπιτρέπειν,
ἀλλὰ τοῦτο αὐτὸ ἐνδείκνυσθαι, ὅτι πολὺ μᾶλλον κατα-
ψηφιεῖσθε τοῦ τὰ ἐλεινὰ ταῦτα δράματα εἰσάγοντος
καὶ καταγέλαστον τὴν πόλιν ποιοῦντος ἢ τοῦ ἡσυχίαν
10 ἄγοντος.
Χωρὶς δὲ τῆς δόξης, ὦ ἄνδρες, οὐδὲ δίκαιόν μοι δοκεῖ
C εἶναι δεῖσθαι τοῦ δικαστοῦ οὐδὲ δεόμενον ἀποφεύγειν,
ἀλλὰ διδάσκειν καὶ πείθειν. οὐ γὰρ ἐπὶ τούτῳ κάθηται

ὁ δικαστής, ἐπὶ τῷ καταχαρίζεσθαι τὰ δίκαια, ἀλλ' ἐπὶ
τῷ κρίνειν ταῦτα· καὶ ὀμώμοκεν οὐ χαριεῖσθαι οἷς ἂν
δοκῇ αὐτῷ, ἀλλὰ δικάσειν κατὰ τοὺς νόμους. οὔκουν 5
χρὴ οὔτε ἡμᾶς ἐθίζειν ὑμᾶς ἐπιορκεῖν οὔθ' ὑμᾶς ἐθίζε-
σθαι· οὐδέτεροι γὰρ ἂν ἡμῶν εὐσεβοῖεν. μὴ οὖν ἀξιοῦ-
τέ με, ὦ ἄνδρες Ἀθηναῖοι, τοιαῦτα δεῖν πρὸς ὑμᾶς
πράττειν ἃ μήτε ἡγοῦμαι καλὰ εἶναι μήτε δίκαια μήτε D
ὅσια, ἄλλως τε μέντοι νὴ Δία πάντως καὶ ἀσεβείας
φεύγοντα ὑπὸ Μελήτου τουτουΐ. σαφῶς γὰρ ἄν, εἰ
πείθοιμι ὑμᾶς καὶ τῷ δεῖσθαι βιαζοίμην ὀμωμοκότας,
θεοὺς ἂν διδάσκοιμι μὴ ἡγεῖσθαι ὑμᾶς εἶναι, καὶ ἀτεχνῶς 5
ἀπολογούμενος κατηγοροίην ἂν ἐμαυτοῦ ὡς θεοὺς οὐ
νομίζω. ἀλλὰ πολλοῦ δεῖ οὕτως ἔχειν· νομίζω τε γάρ,
ὦ ἄνδρες Ἀθηναῖοι, ὡς οὐδεὶς τῶν ἐμῶν κατηγόρων, καὶ
ὑμῖν ἐπιτρέπω καὶ τῷ θεῷ κρῖναι περὶ ἐμοῦ ὅπῃ μέλλει
ἐμοί τε ἄριστα εἶναι καὶ ὑμῖν.   10

SECOND SPEECH

*Socrates has to propose an alternative penalty to that of his
accusers, death.*

There are many reasons why I am not grieved, O 36
men of Athens, at the vote of condemnation. I expected it, and am only surprised that the votes are
so nearly equal; for I had thought that the majority
against me would have been far larger; but now, had 5
thirty votes gone over to the other side, I should have
been acquitted. And I may say, I think, that I have
escaped Meletus. I may say more; for without the
assistance of Anytus and Lycon, any one may see that
he would not have had a fifth part of the votes, as 10
the law requires, in which case he would have incurred B
a fine of a thousand drachmae.

And so he proposes death as the penalty. And
what shall I propose on my part, O men of Athens?
Clearly that which is my due. And what is my due? 5
What return shall be made to the man who has never
had the wit to be idle during his whole life; but has

been careless of what the many care for—wealth, and
family interests, and military offices, and speaking in
10 the assembly, and magistracies, and plots, and parties.
c Reflecting that I was really too honest a man to be
a politician and live, I did not go where I could do
no good to you or to myself; but where I could do the
greatest good privately to every one of you, thither
5 I went, and sought to persuade every man among you
that he must look to himself, and seek virtue and
wisdom before he looks to his private interests, and
look to the state before he looks to the interests of
the state; and that this should be the order which
D he observes in all his actions.   What shall be done to
such an one?   Doubtless some good thing, O men of
Athens, if he has his reward; and the good should
be of a kind suitable to him.   What would be a reward
5 suitable to a poor man who is your benefactor, and
who desires leisure that he may instruct you?   There
can be no reward so fitting as maintenance in the
Prytaneum, O men of Athens, a reward which he
deserves far more than the citizen who has won the
10 prize at Olympia in the horse or chariot race, whether
the chariots were drawn by two horses or by many.
E For I am in want, and he has enough; and he only
gives you the appearance of happiness, and I give you
the reality.   And if I am to estimate the penalty fairly,
37 I should say that maintenance in the Prytaneum is the
just return.

*Socrates is convinced that he will be doing wrong to himself,
if he proposes any penalty which the court would consider
adequate.*

Perhaps you think that I am braving you in what
I am saying now, as in what I said before about the
5 tears and prayers.   But this is not so.   I speak rather
because I am convinced that I never intentionally
wronged any one, although I cannot convince you—
the time has been too short; if there were a law at
Athens, as there is in other cities, that a capital cause
B should not be decided in one day, then I believe that
I should have convinced you.   But I cannot in a moment
refute great slanders; and, as I am convinced that

I never wronged another, I will assuredly not wrong
myself. I will not say of myself that I deserve any 5
evil, or propose any penalty. Why should I? Because
I am afraid of the penalty of death which Meletus
proposes? When I do not know whether death is a
good or an evil, why should I propose a penalty which
would certainly be an evil? Shall I say imprisonment? 10
And why should I live in prison, and be the slave of c
the magistrates of the year—of the Eleven? Or shall
the penalty be a fine, and imprisonment until the fine
is paid? There is the same objection. I should have
to lie in prison, for money I have none, and cannot 5
pay.

*He will not propose banishment. What the Athenians could
not endure, no other city will, and he is forbidden to keep silent.*

Ἀλλὰ δὴ φυγῆς τιμήσωμαι; ἴσως γὰρ ἄν μοι τούτου
τιμήσαιτε. πολλὴ μεντἄν με φιλοψυχία ἔχοι, ὦ
ἄνδρες Ἀθηναῖοι, εἰ οὕτως ἀλόγιστός εἰμι ὥστε μὴ
δύνασθαι λογίζεσθαι ὅτι ὑμεῖς μὲν ὄντες πολῖταί μου 10
οὐχ οἷοί τε ἐγένεσθε ἐνεγκεῖν τὰς ἐμὰς διατριβὰς καὶ
τοὺς λόγους, ἀλλ' ὑμῖν βαρύτεραι γεγόνασιν καὶ ἐπι-
φθονώτεραι, ὥστε ζητεῖτε αὐτῶν νυνὶ ἀπαλλαγῆναι· D
ἄλλοι δὲ ἄρα αὐτὰς οἴσουσι ῥᾳδίως; πολλοῦ γε δεῖ,
ὦ ἄνδρες Ἀθηναῖοι. καλὸς οὖν ἄν μοι ὁ βίος εἴη
ἐξελθόντι τηλικῷδε ἀνθρώπῳ ἄλλην ἐξ ἄλλης πόλεως
ἀμειβομένῳ καὶ ἐξελαυνομένῳ ζῆν. εὖ γὰρ οἶδ' ὅτι 5
ὅποι ἂν ἔλθω, λέγοντος ἐμοῦ ἀκροάσονται οἱ νέοι ὥσπερ
ἐνθάδε· κἂν μὲν τούτους ἀπελαύνω, οὗτοί με αὐτοὶ ἐξε-
λῶσι πείθοντες τοὺς πρεσβυτέρους· ἐὰν δὲ μὴ ἀπελαύνω, E
οἱ τούτων πατέρες δὲ καὶ οἰκεῖοι δι' αὐτοὺς τούτους.

Ἴσως οὖν ἄν τις εἴποι· " Σιγῶν δὲ καὶ ἡσυχίαν
ἄγων, ὦ Σώκρατες, οὐχ οἷός τ' ἔσῃ ἡμῖν ἐξελθὼν ζῆν; "
τουτὶ δή ἐστι πάντων χαλεπώτατον πεῖσαί τινας ὑμῶν. 5
ἐάντε γὰρ λέγω ὅτι τῷ θεῷ ἀπειθεῖν τοῦτ' ἐστὶν καὶ διὰ
τοῦτ' ἀδύνατον ἡσυχίαν ἄγειν, οὐ πείσεσθέ μοι ὡς εἰρω- 38
νευομένῳ· ἐάντ' αὖ λέγω ὅτι καὶ τυγχάνει μέγιστον

ἀγαθὸν ὂν ἀνθρώπῳ τοῦτο, ἑκάστης ἡμέρας περὶ ἀρετῆς
τοὺς λόγους ποιεῖσθαι καὶ τῶν ἄλλων περὶ ὧν ὑμεῖς
5 ἐμοῦ ἀκούετε διαλεγομένου καὶ ἐμαυτὸν καὶ ἄλλους
ἐξετάζοντος, ὁ δὲ ἀνεξέταστος βίος οὐ βιωτὸς ἀνθρώπῳ,
ταῦτα δ᾽ ἔτι ἧττον πείσεσθέ μοι λέγοντι. τὰ δὲ ἔχει
μὲν οὕτως, ὡς ἐγώ φημι, ὦ ἄνδρες, πείθειν δὲ οὐ ῥᾴδιον.
καὶ ἐγὼ ἅμα οὐκ εἴθισμαι ἐμαυτὸν ἀξιοῦν κακοῦ οὐδενός.
B εἰ μὲν γὰρ ἦν μοι χρήματα, ἐτιμησάμην ἂν χρημάτων
ὅσα ἔμελλον ἐκτείσειν, οὐδὲν γὰρ ἂν ἐβλάβην· νῦν δὲ
οὐ γὰρ ἔστιν, εἰ μὴ ἄρα ὅσον ἂν ἐγὼ δυναίμην ἐκτεῖσαι,
τοσούτου βούλεσθέ μοι τιμῆσαι. ἴσως δ᾽ ἂν δυναίμην
5 ἐκτεῖσαι ὑμῖν που μνᾶν ἀργυρίου· τοσούτου οὖν τιμῶμαι.

Πλάτων δὲ ὅδε, ὦ ἄνδρες Ἀθηναῖοι, καὶ Κρίτων καὶ
Κριτόβουλος καὶ Ἀπολλόδωρος κελεύουσί με τριάκοντα
μνῶν τιμήσασθαι, αὐτοὶ δ᾽ ἐγγυᾶσθαι· τιμῶμαι οὖν
τοσούτου, ἐγγυηταὶ δὲ ὑμῖν ἔσονται τοῦ ἀργυρίου οὗτοι
10 ἀξιόχρεῳ.

THIRD SPEECH

*Address of Socrates to the court after the ratification of the
death-sentence.*

c Not much time will be gained, O Athenians, in
return for the evil name which you will get from the
detractors of the city, who will say that you killed
Socrates, a wise man ; for they will call me wise, even
5 although I am not wise, when they want to reproach
you. If you had waited a little while, your desire
would have been fulfilled in the course of nature. For
I am far advanced in years, as you may perceive, and
not far from death. I am speaking now not to all of
D you, but only to those who have condemned me to death.
And I have another thing to say to them : You think
that I was convicted because I had no words of the
sort which would have procured my acquittal—I mean
5 if I had thought fit to leave nothing undone or unsaid.
Not so; the deficiency which led to my conviction
was not of words—certainly not. But I had not the

boldness or impudence or inclination to address you as
you would have liked me to do, weeping and wailing
and lamenting, and saying and doing many things which E
you have been accustomed to hear from others, and
which, as I maintain, are unworthy of me. I thought
at the time that I ought not to do anything common
or mean when in danger: nor do I now repent of 5
the style of my defence; I would rather die having
spoken after my manner, than speak in your manner
and live. For neither in war nor yet at law ought
I or any man to use every way of escaping death. 39
Often in battle there can be no doubt that if a man will
throw away his arms, and fall on his knees before his
pursuers, he may escape death; and in other dangers
there are other ways of escaping death, if a man is 5
willing to say and do anything. The difficulty, my
friends, is not to avoid death, but to avoid unrighteousness; for that runs faster than death. I am old and B
move slowly, and the slower runner has overtaken me,
and my accusers are keen and quick, and the faster
runner, who is unrighteousness, has overtaken them.
And now I depart hence condemned by you to suffer 5
the penalty of death,—they too go their ways condemned by the truth to suffer the penalty of villainy
and wrong; and I must abide by my reward—let them
abide by theirs. I suppose that these things may be
regarded as fated—and I think that they are well.   10

His mission will be carried on by others after him, so that the
Athenians will not achieve their aims by the mere execution of
a death-sentence.

Τὸ δὲ δὴ μετὰ τοῦτο ἐπιθυμῶ ὑμῖν χρησμῳδῆσαι, C
ὦ καταψηφισάμενοί μου· καὶ γάρ εἰμι ἤδη ἐνταῦθα ἐν
ᾧ μάλιστα ἄνθρωποι χρησμῳδοῦσιν, ὅταν μέλλωσιν
ἀποθανεῖσθαι. φημὶ γάρ, ὦ ἄνδρες οἳ ἐμὲ ἀπεκτόνατε,
τιμωρίαν ὑμῖν ἥξειν εὐθὺς μετὰ τὸν ἐμὸν θάνατον πολὺ 5
χαλεπωτέραν νὴ Δία ἢ οἵαν ἐμὲ ἀπεκτόνατε· νῦν γὰρ
τοῦτο εἴργασθε οἰόμενοι μὲν ἀπαλλάξεσθαι τοῦ διδόναι
ἔλεγχον τοῦ βίου, τὸ δὲ ὑμῖν πολὺ ἐναντίον ἀποβήσεται,
ὡς ἐγώ φημι. πλείους ἔσονται ὑμᾶς οἱ ἐλέγχοντες, D

οὓς νῦν ἐγὼ κατεῖχον, ὑμεῖς δὲ οὐκ ᾐσθάνεσθε· καὶ
χαλεπώτεροι ἔσονται ὅσῳ νεώτεροί εἰσιν, καὶ ὑμεῖς
μᾶλλον ἀγανακτήσετε. εἰ γὰρ οἴεσθε ἀποκτείνοντες
5 ἀνθρώπους ἐπισχήσειν τοῦ ὀνειδίζειν τινὰ ὑμῖν ὅτι
οὐκ ὀρθῶς ζῆτε, οὐ καλῶς διανοεῖσθε· οὐ γάρ ἐσθ᾽
αὕτη ἡ ἀπαλλαγὴ οὔτε πάνυ δυνατὴ οὔτε καλή, ἀλλ᾽
ἐκείνη καὶ καλλίστη καὶ ῥᾴστη, μὴ τοὺς ἄλλους
κολούειν ἀλλ᾽ ἑαυτὸν παρασκευάζειν ὅπως ἔσται ὡς
10 βέλτιστος. ταῦτα μὲν οὖν ὑμῖν τοῖς καταψηφισαμένοις μαντευσάμενος ἀπαλλάττομαι.

*To those who voted for his acquittal he explains his reasons
for the conviction that nothing but good awaits him.*

E Friends, who would have acquitted me, I would like
also to talk with you about the thing which has come
to pass, while the magistrates are busy, and before I go
to the place at which I must die. Stay then a little, for
5 we may as well talk with one another while there is
40 time. You are my friends, and I should like to show
you the meaning of this event which has happened
to me. O my judges—for you I may truly call judges—
I should like to tell you of a wonderful circumstance.
5 Hitherto the divine faculty of which the internal oracle
is the source has constantly been in the habit of oppos-
ing me even about trifles, if I was going to make a slip
or error in any matter; and now as you see there has
come upon me that which may be thought, and is
10 generally believed to be, the last and worst evil. But
B the oracle made no sign of opposition, either when I
was leaving my house in the morning, or when I was on
my way to the court, or while I was speaking, at anything which I was going to say; and yet I have often
5 been stopped in the middle of a speech, but now in
nothing I either said or did touching the matter in hand
has the oracle opposed me. What do I take to be
the explanation of this silence? I will tell you. It is
an intimation that what has happened to me is a good,
c and that those of us who think that death is an evil
are in error. For the customary sign would surely
have opposed me had I been going to evil and not
to good.

*Death presents alternative prospects, with either of which he
is well satisfied. His mission may yet continue in another
world.*

Let us reflect in another way, and we shall see that 5
there is great reason to hope that death is a good ; for
one of two things—either death is a state of nothing-
ness and utter unconsciousness, or, as men say, there
is a change and migration of the soul from this world
to another. Now if you suppose that there is no con- 10
sciousness, but a sleep like the sleep of him who is D
undisturbed even by dreams, death will be an unspeak-
able gain. For if a person were to select the night in
which his sleep was undisturbed even by dreams, and
were to compare with this the other days and nights 5
of his life, and then were to tell us how many days and
nights he had passed in the course of his life better and
more pleasantly than this one, I think that any man,
I will not say a private man, but even the great king,
will not find many such days or nights, when com- E
pared with the others. Now if death be of such a nature,
I say that to die is gain ; for eternity is then only
a single night. But if death is the journey to another
place, and there, as men say, all the dead abide, what 5
good, O my friends and judges, can be greater than
this ? If indeed when the pilgrim arrives in the world
below, he is delivered from the professors of justice in 41
this world, and finds the true judges who are said to
give judgement there, Minos and Rhadamanthus and
Aeacus and Triptolemus, and other sons of God who
were righteous in their own life, that pilgrimage will be 5
worth making. What would not a man give if he
might converse with Orpheus and Musaeus and Hesiod
and Homer ? Nay, if this be true, let me die again
and again. I myself, too, shall have a wonderful interest in there meeting and conversing with Palamedes, B
and Ajax the son of Telamon, and any other ancient
hero who has suffered death through an unjust judgement ; and there will be no small pleasure, as I think,
in comparing my own sufferings with theirs. Above 5
all, I shall then be able to continue my search into true
and false knowledge ; as in this world, so also in the

next; and I shall find out who is wise, and who pre-
tends to be wise, and is not.   What would not a man
10 give, O judges, to be able to examine the leader of the
c great Trojan expedition; or Odysseus or Sisyphus,
or numberless others, men and women too ! What
infinite delight would there be in conversing with them
and asking them questions ! In another world they do
5 not put a man to death for asking questions : assuredly
not. For besides being happier than we are, they will
be immortal, if what is said is true.

*God permits no good man to suffer real harm, whether in life
er death.*

Ἀλλὰ καὶ ὑμᾶς χρή, ὦ ἄνδρες δικασταί, εὐέλπιδας
εἶναι πρὸς τὸν θάνατον, καὶ ἕν τι τοῦτο διανοεῖσθαι
D ἀληθές, ὅτι οὐκ ἔστιν ἀνδρὶ ἀγαθῷ κακὸν οὐδὲν οὔτε
ζῶντι οὔτε τελευτήσαντι, οὐδὲ ἀμελεῖται ὑπὸ θεῶν τὰ
τούτου πράγματα· οὐδὲ τὰ ἐμὰ νῦν ἀπὸ τοῦ αὐτομάτου
γέγονεν, ἀλλά μοι δῆλόν ἐστι τοῦτο, ὅτι ἤδη τεθνάναι
5 καὶ ἀπηλλάχθαι πραγμάτων βέλτιον ἦν μοι.   διὰ
τοῦτο καὶ ἐμὲ οὐδαμοῦ ἀπέτρεψεν τὸ σημεῖον, καὶ
ἔγωγε τοῖς καταψηφισαμένοις μου καὶ τοῖς κατηγόροις
οὐ πάνυ χαλεπαίνω.   καίτοι οὐ ταύτῃ τῇ διανοίᾳ κατε-
ψηφίζοντό μου καὶ κατηγόρουν, ἀλλ᾽ οἰόμενοι βλάπτειν·
E τοῦτο αὐτοῖς ἄξιον μέμφεσθαι.   τοσόνδε μέντοι αὐτῶν
δέομαι· τοὺς ὑεῖς μου, ἐπειδὰν ἡβήσωσι, τιμωρήσασθε,
ὦ ἄνδρες, ταὐτὰ ταῦτα λυποῦντες ἅπερ ἐγὼ ὑμᾶς
ἐλύπουν, ἐὰν ὑμῖν δοκῶσιν ἢ χρημάτων ἢ ἄλλου του
5 πρότερον ἐπιμελεῖσθαι ἢ ἀρετῆς, καὶ ἐὰν δοκῶσί τι
εἶναι μηδὲν ὄντες, ὀνειδίζετε αὐτοῖς ὥσπερ ἐγὼ ὑμῖν,
ὅτι οὐκ ἐπιμελοῦνται ὧν δεῖ, καὶ οἴονταί τι εἶναι ὄντες
42 οὐδενὸς ἄξιοι.   καὶ ἐὰν ταῦτα ποιῆτε, δίκαια πεπονθὼς
ἐγὼ ἔσομαι ὑφ᾽ ὑμῶν αὐτός τε καὶ οἱ ὑεῖς.   ἀλλὰ γὰρ
ἤδη ὥρα ἀπιέναι, ἐμοὶ μὲν ἀποθανουμένῳ, ὑμῖν δὲ
βιωσομένοις· ὁπότεροι δὲ ἡμῶν ἔρχονται ἐπὶ ἄμεινον
5 πρᾶγμα, ἄδηλον παντὶ πλὴν εἰ τῷ θεῷ.

SCENE II. SOCRATES IN PRISON

Crito, coming early to visit Socrates, finds him quite unmoved by the thought of his approaching death.

ΣΩ. Τί τηνικάδε ἀφῖξαι, ὦ Κρίτων; ἢ οὐ πρῷ ἔτι 43 ἐστίν;

ΚΡ. Πάνυ μὲν οὖν.

ΣΩ. Πηνίκα μάλιστα;

ΚΡ. Ὄρθρος βαθύς. 5

ΣΩ. Θαυμάζω ὅπως ἠθέλησέ σοι ὁ τοῦ δεσμωτηρίου φύλαξ ὑπακοῦσαι.

ΚΡ. Συνήθης ἤδη μοί ἐστιν, ὦ Σώκρατες, διὰ τὸ πολλάκις δεῦρο φοιτᾶν, καί τι καὶ εὐεργέτηται ὑπ᾿ ἐμοῦ.

ΣΩ. Ἄρτι δὲ ἥκεις ἢ πάλαι; 10

ΚΡ. Ἐπιεικῶς πάλαι.

ΣΩ. Εἶτα πῶς οὐκ εὐθὺς ἐπήγειράς με, ἀλλὰ σιγῇ B παρακάθησαι;

ΚΡ. Οὐ μὰ τὸν Δία, ὦ Σώκρατες, οὐδ᾿ ἂν αὐτὸς ἤθελον ἐν τοσαύτῃ τε ἀγρυπνίᾳ καὶ λύπῃ εἶναι, ἀλλὰ καὶ σοῦ πάλαι θαυμάζω αἰσθανόμενος ὡς ἡδέως καθεύ- 5 δεις. καὶ ἐπίτηδές σε οὐκ ἤγειρον ἵνα ὡς ἥδιστα διάγῃς. καὶ πολλάκις μὲν δή σε καὶ πρότερον ἐν παντὶ τῷ βίῳ ηὐδαιμόνισα τοῦ τρόπου, πολὺ δὲ μάλιστα ἐν τῇ νῦν παρεστώσῃ συμφορᾷ, ὡς ῥᾳδίως αὐτὴν καὶ πρᾴως φέρεις. 10

ΣΩ. Καὶ γὰρ ἄν, ὦ Κρίτων, πλημμελὲς εἴη ἀγανα-κτεῖν τηλικοῦτον ὄντα εἰ δεῖ ἤδη τελευτᾶν.

ΚΡ. Καὶ ἄλλοι, ὦ Σώκρατες, τηλικοῦτοι ἐν τοιαύταις C συμφοραῖς ἁλίσκονται, ἀλλ᾿ οὐδὲν αὐτοὺς ἐπιλύεται ἡ ἡλικία τὸ μὴ οὐχὶ ἀγανακτεῖν τῇ παρούσῃ τύχῃ.

ΣΩ. Ἔστι ταῦτα. ἀλλὰ τί δὴ οὕτω πρῷ ἀφῖξαι;

The mission-ship has been sighted off Sunium. Socrates narrates his dream.

ΚΡ. Ἀγγελίαν, ὦ Σώκρατες, φέρων χαλεπήν, οὐ σοί, 5

ὡς ἐμοὶ φαίνεται, ἀλλ' ἐμοὶ καὶ τοῖς σοῖς ἐπιτηδείοις
πᾶσιν καὶ χαλεπὴν καὶ βαρεῖαν, ἣν ἐγώ, ὡς ἐμοὶ δοκῶ,
ἐν τοῖς βαρύτατ' ἂν ἐνέγκαιμι.

ΣΩ. Τίνα ταύτην; ἢ τὸ πλοῖον ἀφῖκται ἐκ Δήλου,
D οὗ δεῖ ἀφικομένου τεθνάναι με;

ΚΡ. Οὔτοι δὴ ἀφῖκται, ἀλλὰ δοκεῖ μέν μοι ἥξειν
τήμερον ἐξ ὧν ἀπαγγέλλουσιν ἥκοντές τινες ἀπὸ
Σουνίου καὶ καταλιπόντες ἐκεῖ αὐτό. δῆλον οὖν ἐκ
5 τούτων τῶν ἀγγέλων ὅτι ἥξει τήμερον, καὶ ἀνάγκη δὴ
εἰς αὔριον ἔσται, ὦ Σώκρατες, τὸν βίον σε τελευτᾶν.

ΣΩ. Ἀλλ', ὦ Κρίτων, τύχῃ ἀγαθῇ, εἰ ταύτῃ τοῖς
θεοῖς φίλον, ταύτῃ ἔστω· οὐ μέντοι οἶμαι ἥξειν αὐτὸ
τήμερον.

44 ΚΡ. Πόθεν τοῦτο τεκμαίρῃ;

ΣΩ. Ἐγώ σοι ἐρῶ. τῇ γάρ που ὑστεραίᾳ δεῖ με
ἀποθνήσκειν ἢ ᾗ ἂν ἔλθῃ τὸ πλοῖον.

ΚΡ. Φασί γέ τοι δὴ οἱ τούτων κύριοι.

5 ΣΩ. Οὐ τοίνυν τῆς ἐπιούσης ἡμέρας οἶμαι αὐτὸ
ἥξειν ἀλλὰ τῆς ἑτέρας. τεκμαίρομαι δὲ ἔκ τινος ἐνυπνίου ὃ ἑώρακα ὀλίγον πρότερον ταύτης τῆς νυκτός·
καὶ κινδυνεύεις ἐν καιρῷ τινι οὐκ ἐγεῖραί με.

ΚΡ. Ἦν δὲ δὴ τί τὸ ἐνύπνιον;

10 ΣΩ. Ἐδόκει τίς μοι γυνὴ προσελθοῦσα καλὴ καὶ
B εὐειδής, λευκὰ ἱμάτια ἔχουσα, καλέσαι με καὶ εἰπεῖν·
"Ὦ Σώκρατες, ἤματί κεν τριτάτῳ Φθίην ἐρίβωλον
ἵκοιο."

ΚΡ. Ἄτοπον τὸ ἐνύπνιον, ὦ Σώκρατες.

5 ΣΩ. Ἐναργὲς μὲν οὖν, ὥς γέ μοι δοκεῖ, ὦ Κρίτων.

ΚΡ. Λίαν γε, ὡς ἔοικεν.

*Crito implores Socrates to escape while there is time : if bribery
should be necessary, funds are available.*

Cr. But oh! my beloved Socrates, let me entreat you
once more to take my advice and escape. For if you
die I shall not only lose a friend who can never be

replaced, but there is another evil : people who do not 10
know you and me will believe that I might have saved c
you if I had been willing to give money, but that I did
not care. Now, can there be a worse disgrace than
this—that I should be thought to value money more
than the life of a friend? For the many will not be 5
persuaded that I wanted you to escape, and that you
refused.

Soc. But why, my dear Crito, should we care about
the opinion of the many? Good men, and they are the
only persons who are worth considering, will think of 10
these things truly as they occurred.

Cr. But you see, Socrates, that the opinion of the
many must be regarded, for what is now happening D
shows that they can do the greatest evil to any one who
has lost their good opinion.

Soc. I only wish it were so, Crito ; and that the many
could do the greatest evil ; for then they would also be 5
able to do the greatest good—and what a fine thing this
would be! But in reality they can do neither ; for
they cannot make a man either wise or foolish ; and
whatever they do is the result of chance.

Cr. Well, I will not dispute with you ; but please to E
tell me, Socrates, whether you are not acting out of
regard to me and your other friends : are you not afraid
that if you escape from prison we may get into trouble
with the informers for having stolen you away, and lose 5
either the whole or a great part of our property ; or
that even a worse evil may happen to us? Now, if you
fear on our account, be at ease ; for in order to save 45
you, we ought surely to run this, or even a greater risk ;
be persuaded then, and do as I say.

Soc. Yes, Crito, that is one fear which you mention,
but by no means the only one. 5

Cr. Fear not—there are persons who are willing to
get you out of prison at no great cost ; and as for the
informers, they are far from being exorbitant in their
demands—a little money will satisfy them. My means,
which are certainly ample, are at your service, and if B
you have a scruple about spending all mine, here are
strangers who will give you the use of theirs ; and one
of them, Simmias the Theban, has brought a large sum

5 of money for this very purpose ; and Cebes and many others are prepared to spend their money in helping you to escape.

Crito offers Socrates a home with friends in Thessaly : he must not desert his sons, nor disgrace his friends in the eyes of the world, as he will by refusing to accept their offer.

Cr. I say, therefore, do not hesitate on our account, and do not say, as you did in the court, that you will 10 have a difficulty in knowing what to do with yourself anywhere else. For men will love you in other places c to which you may go, and not in Athens only; there are friends of mine in Thessaly, if you like to go to them, who will value and protect you, and no Thessalian will give you any trouble. Nor can I think that you are 5 at all justified, Socrates, in betraying your own life, when you might be saved ; in acting thus you are playing into the hands of your enemies, who are hurry-ing on your destruction. And further I should say d that you are deserting your own children ; for you might bring them up and educate them ; instead of which you go away and leave them, and they will have to take their chance ; and if they do not meet with the 5 usual fate of orphans, there will be small thanks to you. No man should bring children into the world who is unwilling to persevere to the end in their nurture and education. But you appear to be choosing the easier part, not the better and manlier, which would have been 10 more becoming in one who professes to care for virtue in all his actions, like yourself. And indeed, I am e ashamed not only of you, but of us who are your friends, when I reflect that the whole business will be attributed entirely to our want of courage. The trial need never have come on, or might have been managed differently ; 5 and this last act, or crowning folly, will seem to have occurred through our negligence and cowardice, who 46 might have saved you, if we had been good for anything ; and you might have saved yourself, for there was no difficulty at all. See now, Socrates, how sad and dis-creditable are the consequences, both to us and you. 5 Make up your mind then, or rather have your mind already made up, for the time of deliberation is over, and

there is only one thing to be done, which must be done
this very night, and if we delay at all will be no longer
practicable or possible: I beseech you therefore, Socrates,
be persuaded by me, and do as I say. 10

*Socrates avers that he must listen to the voice of reason, as he
has always done, and not to popular opinion, and invites Crito
to consider the question with him.*

ΣΩ. 'Ω φίλε Κρίτων, ἡ προθυμία σου πολλοῦ ἀξία, B
εἰ μετά τινος ὀρθότητος εἴη· εἰ δὲ μή, ὅσῳ μείζων,
τοσούτῳ χαλεπωτέρα. σκοπεῖσθαι οὖν χρὴ ἡμᾶς, εἴτε
ταῦτα πρακτέον εἴτε μή· ὡς ἐγὼ οὐ μόνον νῦν ἀλλὰ καὶ
ἀεὶ τοιοῦτος, οἷος τῶν ἐμῶν μηδενὶ ἄλλῳ πείθεσθαι ἢ τῷ 5
λόγῳ, ὃς ἄν μοι λογιζομένῳ βέλτιστος φαίνηται. τοὺς
δὲ λόγους, οὓς ἐν τῷ ἔμπροσθεν ἔλεγον, οὐ δύναμαι νῦν
ἐκβαλεῖν, ἐπειδή μοι ἥδε ἡ τύχη γέγονεν, ἀλλὰ σχεδόν
τι ὅμοιοι φαίνονταί μοι, καὶ τοὺς αὐτοὺς πρεσβεύω καὶ C
τιμῶ οὕσπερ καὶ πρότερον· ὧν ἐὰν μὴ βελτίω ἔχωμεν
λέγειν ἐν τῷ παρόντι, εὖ ἴσθι ὅτι οὐ μή σοι ξυγχωρήσω,
οὐδ' ἂν πλείω τῶν νῦν παρόντων ἢ τῶν πολλῶν δύναμις
ὥσπερ παῖδας ἡμᾶς μορμολύττηται, δεσμοὺς καὶ θανά- 5
τους ἐπιπέμπουσα καὶ χρημάτων ἀφαιρέσεις. πῶς οὖν
ἂν μετριώτατα σκοποίμεθα αὐτά; εἰ πρῶτον μὲν τοῦτον
τὸν λόγον ἀναλάβοιμεν, ὃν σὺ λέγεις περὶ τῶν δοξῶν,
πότερον καλῶς ἐλέγετο ἑκάστοτε ἢ οὔ, ὅτι ταῖς μὲν δεῖ
τῶν δοξῶν προσέχειν τὸν νοῦν, ταῖς δὲ οὔ· ἢ πρὶν μὲν D
ἐμὲ δεῖν ἀποθνήσκειν καλῶς ἐλέγετο, νῦν δὲ κατάδηλος
ἄρα ἐγένετο ὅτι ἄλλως ἕνεκα λόγου ἐλέγετο, ἦν δὲ
παιδιὰ καὶ φλυαρία ὡς ἀληθῶς; ἐπιθυμῶ δ' ἔγωγ' ἐπι-
σκέψασθαι, ὦ Κρίτων, κοινῇ μετὰ σοῦ εἰ τί μοι ἀλλοιό- 5
τερος φανεῖται, ἐπειδὴ ὧδε ἔχω, ἢ ὁ αὐτός, καὶ ἐάσομεν
χαίρειν ἢ πεισόμεθα αὐτῷ. ἐλέγετο δέ πως, ὡς ἐγᾦμαι,
ἑκάστοτε ὧδε ὑπὸ τῶν οἰομένων τὶ λέγειν, ὥσπερ νυνδὴ
ἐγὼ ἔλεγον, ὅτι τῶν δοξῶν ἃς οἱ ἄνθρωποι δοξάζουσιν
δέοι τὰς μὲν περὶ πολλοῦ ποιεῖσθαι, τὰς δὲ μή. τοῦτο E
πρὸς θεῶν, ὦ Κρίτων, οὐ δοκεῖ καλῶς σοι λέγεσθαι;

—σὺ γάρ, ὅσα γε τἀνθρώπεια, ἐκτὸς εἶ τοῦ μέλλειν
47 ἀποθνῄσκειν αὔριον, καὶ οὐκ ἂν σὲ παρακρούοι ἡ
παροῦσα συμφορά· σκόπει δή—οὐχ ἱκανῶς δοκεῖ σοι
λέγεσθαι ὅτι οὐ πάσας χρὴ τὰς δόξας τῶν ἀνθρώπων
5 τιμᾶν ἀλλὰ τὰς μέν, τὰς δ' οὔ, οὐδὲ πάντων ἀλλὰ τῶν
μέν, τῶν δ' οὔ; τί φῄς; ταῦτα οὐχὶ καλῶς λέγεται;
    ΚΡ. Καλῶς.
    ΣΩ. Οὐκοῦν τὰς μὲν χρηστὰς τιμᾶν, τὰς δὲ πονηρὰς
μή·
    ΚΡ. Ναί.
10 ΣΩ. Χρησταὶ δὲ οὐχ αἱ τῶν φρονίμων, πονηραὶ δὲ
αἱ τῶν ἀφρόνων;
    ΚΡ. Πῶς δ' οὔ;

*The analogy of the athlete in training, who follows expert
advice, shows that in living the good life we must not follow the
opinion of the many. All that remains is to consider whether
it is right to attempt to escape.*

Soc. And what was said about another matter? Is
B the pupil who devotes himself to the practice of gym-
nastics supposed to attend to the praise and blame and
opinion of every man, or of one man only—his physician
or trainer, whoever he may be?
5   Cr. Of one man only.
Soc. And he ought to fear the censure and welcome
the praise of that one only, and not of the many?
Cr. Clearly so.
Soc. And he ought to act and train, and eat and
10 drink in the way which seems good to his single master
who has understanding, rather than according to the
opinion of all other men put together?
Cr. True.
c Soc. And if he disobeys and disregards the opinion
and approval of the one, and regards the opinion of the
many who have no understanding, will he not suffer
evil?
5   Cr. Certainly he will.
Soc. And what will the evil be, whither tending and
what affecting, in the disobedient person?

Cr. Clearly, affecting the body; that is what is destroyed by the evil.

Soc. Very good; and is not this true, Crito, of other 10 things which we need not separately enumerate? In questions of just and unjust, fair and foul, good and evil, which are the subjects of our present consultation, ought we to follow the opinion of the many and to fear them; D or the opinion of the one man who has understanding? ought we not to fear and reverence him more than all the rest of the world: and if we desert him shall we not destroy and injure that principle in us which may be 5 assumed to be improved by justice and deteriorated by injustice—there is such a principle?

Cr. Certainly there is, Socrates.

Soc. Take a parallel instance :—if, acting under the advice of those who have no understanding, we destroy 10 that which is improved by health and is deteriorated by disease, would life be worth having? And that which E has been destroyed is—the body?

Cr. Yes.

Soc. Could we live, having an evil and corrupted body? 5

Cr. Certainly not.

Soc. And will life be worth having, if that higher part of man be destroyed, which is improved by justice and depraved by injustice? Do we suppose that principle, whatever it may be in man, which has to do with justice 10 and injustice, to be inferior to the body? 48

Cr. Certainly not.

Soc. More honourable than the body?

Cr. Far more.

Soc. Then, my friend, we must not regard what the 5 many say of us: but what he, the one man who has understanding of just and unjust, will say, and what the truth will say. And therefore you begin in error when you advise that we should regard the opinion of the many about just and unjust, good and evil, honourable 10 and dishonourable.—'Well,' some one will say, 'but the many can kill us.'

Cr. Yes, Socrates; that will clearly be the answer. B

Soc. And it is true: but still I find with surprise that the old argument is unshaken as ever. And I should like to

know whether I may say the same of another proposition
5 —that not life, but a good life, is to be chiefly valued?
Cr. Yes, that also remains unshaken.
Soc. And a good life is equivalent to a just and honourable one—that holds also?
Cr. Yes, it does.
10 *Soc.* From these premises I proceed to argue the question whether I ought or ought not to try and escape
c without the consent of the Athenians: and if I am clearly right in escaping, then I will make the attempt; but if not, I will abstain. The other considerations which you mention, of money and loss of character and
5 the duty of educating one's children, are, I fear, only the doctrines of the multitude, who would be as ready to restore people to life, if they were able, as they are to put them to death—and with as little reason. But now, since the argument has thus far prevailed, the only
10 question which remains to be considered is, whether we
d shall do rightly either in escaping or suffering others to aid in our escape and paying them in money and thanks, or whether in reality we shall not do rightly; and if the latter, then death or any other calamity which
5 may ensue on my remaining here must not be allowed to enter into the calculation.
Cr. I think that you are right, Socrates; how then shall we proceed?
Soc. Let us consider the matter together, and do
10 you either refute me if you can, and I will be convinced;
e or else cease, my dear friend, from repeating to me that I ought to escape against the wishes of the Athenians: for I highly value your attempts to persuade me to do so, but I may not be persuaded against my own better
5 judgement. And now please to consider my first position,
49 and try how you can best answer me.
Cr. I will.

The whole question turns upon the principle that we must never return evil for evil.

ΣΩ. Οὐδενὶ τρόπῳ φαμὲν ἑκόντας ἀδικητέον εἶναι,
ἢ -ινὶ μὲν ἀδικητέον τρόπῳ τινὶ δὲ οὔ: ἢ οὐδαμῶς τό γε
5 ἀδικεῖν οὔτε ἀγαθὸν οὔτε καλόν, ὡς πολλάκις ἡμῖν καὶ

ἐν τῷ ἔμπροσθεν χρόνῳ ὡμολογήθη; ἢ πᾶσαι ἡμῖν
ἐκεῖναι αἱ πρόσθεν ὁμολογίαι ἐν ταῖσδε ταῖς ὀλίγαις
ἡμέραις ἐκκεχυμέναι εἰσίν, καὶ πάλαι, ὦ Κρίτων, ἄρα
τηλικοίδε ἄνδρες πρὸς ἀλλήλους σπουδῇ διαλεγόμενοι
ἐλάθομεν ἡμᾶς αὐτοὺς παίδων οὐδὲν διαφέροντες; B
ἢ παντὸς μᾶλλον οὕτως ἔχει ὥσπερ τότε ἐλέγετο ἡμῖν·
εἴτε φασὶν οἱ πολλοὶ εἴτε μή, καὶ εἴτε δεῖ ἡμᾶς ἔτι
τῶνδε χαλεπώτερα πάσχειν εἴτε καὶ πραότερα, ὅμως τό
γε ἀδικεῖν τῷ ἀδικοῦντι καὶ κακὸν καὶ αἰσχρὸν τυγχάνει 5
ὂν παντὶ τρόπῳ; φαμὲν ἢ οὔ;

ΚΡ. Φαμέν.

ΣΩ. Οὐδαμῶς ἄρα δεῖ ἀδικεῖν.

ΚΡ. Οὐ δῆτα.

ΣΩ. Οὐδὲ ἀδικούμενον ἄρα ἀνταδικεῖν, ὡς οἱ πολλοὶ 10
οἴονται, ἐπειδή γε οὐδαμῶς δεῖ ἀδικεῖν.

ΚΡ. Οὐ φαίνεται.   c

ΣΩ. Τί δὲ δή; κακουργεῖν δεῖ, ὦ Κρίτων, ἢ οὔ;

ΚΡ. Οὐ δεῖ δήπου, ὦ Σώκρατες.

ΣΩ. Τί δέ; ἀντικακουργεῖν κακῶς πάσχοντα, ὡς οἱ
πολλοί φασιν, δίκαιον ἢ οὐ δίκαιον;   5

ΚΡ. Οὐδαμῶς.

ΣΩ. Τὸ γάρ που κακῶς ποιεῖν ἀνθρώπους τοῦ ἀδικεῖν
οὐδὲν διαφέρει.

ΚΡ. Ἀληθῆ λέγεις.

ΣΩ. Οὔτε ἄρα ἀνταδικεῖν δεῖ οὔτε κακῶς ποιεῖν 10
οὐδένα ἀνθρώπων, οὐδ' ἂν ὁτιοῦν πάσχῃ ὑπ' αὐτῶν.
καὶ ὅρα, ὦ Κρίτων, ταῦτα καθομολογῶν, ὅπως μὴ παρὰ
δόξαν ὁμολογῇς· οἶδα γὰρ ὅτι ὀλίγοις τισὶ ταῦτα καὶ D
δοκεῖ καὶ δόξει. οἷς οὖν οὕτω δέδοκται καὶ οἷς μή,
τούτοις οὐκ ἔστι κοινὴ βουλή, ἀλλὰ ἀνάγκη τούτους
ἀλλήλων καταφρονεῖν ὁρῶντας ἀλλήλων τὰ βουλεύματα.
σκόπει δὴ οὖν καὶ σὺ εὖ μάλα πότερον κοινωνεῖς καὶ 5
συνδοκεῖ σοι καὶ ἀρχώμεθα ἐντεῦθεν βουλευόμενοι, ὡς
οὐδέποτε ὀρθῶς ἔχοντος οὔτε τοῦ ἀδικεῖν οὔτε τοῦ ἀντα-

δικεῖν οὔτε κακῶς πάσχοντα ἀμύνεσθαι ἀντιδρῶντα
κακῶς, ἢ ἀφίστασαι καὶ οὐ κοινωνεῖς τῆς ἀρχῆς; ἐμοὶ
E μὲν γὰρ καὶ πάλαι οὕτω καὶ νῦν ἔτι δοκεῖ, σοὶ δὲ εἴ
πῃ ἄλλῃ δέδοκται, λέγε καὶ δίδασκε. εἰ δ᾽ ἐμμένεις
τοῖς πρόσθε, τὸ μετὰ τοῦτο ἄκουε.

KP. Ἀλλ᾽ ἐμμένω τε καὶ συνδοκεῖ μοι· ἀλλὰ λέγε.

*Admitting this principle, it is difficult to know what argument
can be employed to defend an attempt at escape.*

5   *Soc.* Then I will go on to the next point, which may
be put in the form of a question :—Ought a man to do
what he admits to be right, or ought he to betray the
right ?

Cr. He ought to do what he thinks right.

10   *Soc.* But if this is true, what is the application ? In
50 leaving the prison against the will of the Athenians,
do I wrong any ? or rather do I not wrong those whom
I ought least to wrong ? Do I not desert the principles
which were acknowledged by us to be just—what do you
5 say ?

Cr. I cannot tell, Socrates ; for I do not know.

Soc. Then consider the matter in this way :—Imagine
that I am about to play truant (you may call the pro-
ceeding by any name which you like), and the laws and
10 the government come and interrogate me : ' Tell us,
Socrates,' they say ; 'what are you about ? are you not
B going by an act of yours to overturn us—the laws, and
the whole state, as far as in you lies ? Do you imagine
that a state can subsist and not be overthrown, in which
the decisions of law have no power, but are set aside
5 and trampled upon by individuals ?' What will be our
answer, Crito, to these and the like words ? Any one,
and especially a rhetorician, will have a good deal to say
on behalf of the law which requires a sentence to be
carried out. He will argue that this law should not
10 be set aside ; and shall we reply, ' Yes ; but the state
C has injured us and given an unjust sentence.' Suppose
I say that ?

Cr. Very good, Socrates.

*Socrates supposes that the Laws state their view of the case.
They have done much for him, and have a higher claim to his
obedience than any other authority.*

Soc. 'And was that our agreement with you?' the
laws would answer; 'or were you to abide by the sen- 5
tence of the state?' And if I were to express my
astonishment at their words, the laws would probably
add: 'Answer, Socrates, instead of opening your eyes
—you are in the habit of asking and answering questions.
Tell us,—What complaint have you to make against us D
which justifies you in attempting to destroy us and the
state? In the first place did we not bring you into
existence? Your father married your mother by our
aid and begat you. Say whether you have any objec- 5
tion to urge against those of us who regulate marriage?'
None, I should reply. 'Or against those of us who
after birth regulate the nurture and education of children,
in which you also were trained? Were not the laws,
which have the charge of education, right in command- 10
ing your father to train you in music and gymnastic?'
Right, I should reply. 'Well then, since you were E
brought into the world and nurtured and educated by
us, can you deny in the first place that you are our
child and slave, as your fathers were before you?
And if this is true you are not on equal terms with us; 5
nor can you think that you have a right to do to us
what we are doing to you. Would you have any right
to strike or revile or do any other evil to your father
or your master, if you had one, because you have been
struck or reviled by him, or received some other evil 51
at his hands?—you would not say this? And because
we think right to destroy you, do you think that you have
any right to destroy us in return, and your country as
far as in you lies? Will you, O professor of true virtue, 5
pretend that you are justified in this? Has a philosopher
like you failed to discover that our country is more to
be valued and higher and holier far than mother or
father or any ancestor, and more to be regarded in B
the eyes of the gods and of men of understanding?
also to be soothed, and gently and reverently entreated
when angry, even more than a father, and either to be
persuaded, or if not persuaded, to be obeyed? And 5

when we are punished by her, whether with imprisonment or stripes, the punishment is to be endured in
silence ; and if she lead us to wounds or death in
battle, thither we follow as is right ; neither may any
10 one yield or retreat or leave his rank, but whether in battle
or in court of law, or in any other place, he must do
c what his city and his country order him ; or he must
change their view of what is just : and if he may do no
violence to his father or mother, much less may he do
violence to his country.' What answer shall we make to
5 this, Crito ? Do the laws speak truly, or do they not?
Cr. I think that they do.

*The Laws permit a man to leave his country and go elsewhere
if he is not satisfied with them.*

ΣΩ. "Σκόπει τοίνυν, ὦ Σώκρατες," φαῖεν ἂν ἴσως
οἱ νόμοι, " εἰ ἡμεῖς ταῦτα ἀληθῆ λέγομεν, ὅτι οὐ δίκαια
ἡμᾶς ἐπιχειρεῖς δρᾶν ἃ νῦν ἐπιχειρεῖς. ἡμεῖς γάρ σε
10 γεννήσαντες, ἐκθρέψαντες, παιδεύσαντες, μεταδόντες
D ἁπάντων ὧν οἷοί τ' ἦμεν καλῶν σοὶ καὶ τοῖς ἄλλοις
πᾶσιν πολίταις, ὅμως προαγορεύομεν τῷ ἐξουσίαν
πεποιηκέναι Ἀθηναίων τῷ βουλομένῳ, ἐπειδὰν δοκιμασθῇ καὶ ἴδῃ τὰ ἐν τῇ πόλει πράγματα καὶ ἡμᾶς
5 τοὺς νόμους, ᾧ ἂν μὴ ἀρέσκωμεν ἡμεῖς, ἐξεῖναι λαβόντα
τὰ αὑτοῦ ἀπιέναι ὅποι ἂν βούληται. καὶ οὐδεὶς ἡμῶν
τῶν νόμων ἐμποδών ἐστιν οὐδ' ἀπαγορεύει, ἐάντε τις
βούληται ὑμῶν εἰς ἀποικίαν ἰέναι, εἰ μὴ ἀρέσκοιμεν
ἡμεῖς τε καὶ ἡ πόλις, ἐάντε μετοικεῖν ἄλλοσέ ποι
10 ἐλθών, ἰέναι ἐκεῖσε ὅποι ἂν βούληται, ἔχοντα τὰ αὑτοῦ.
E ὃς δ' ἂν ὑμῶν παραμείνῃ, ὁρῶν ὃν τρόπον ἡμεῖς τάς
τε δίκας δικάζομεν καὶ τἆλλα τὴν πόλιν διοικοῦμεν,
ἤδη φαμὲν τοῦτον ὡμολογηκέναι ἔργῳ ἡμῖν ἃ ἂν ἡμεῖς
κελεύωμεν ποιήσειν ταῦτα, καὶ τὸν μὴ πειθόμενον
5 τριχῇ φαμεν ἀδικεῖν, ὅτι τε γεννηταῖς οὖσιν ἡμῖν οὐ
πείθεται, καὶ ὅτι τροφεῦσι, καὶ ὅτι ὁμολογήσας ἡμῖν
πείσεσθαι οὔτε πείθεται οὔτε πείθει ἡμᾶς, εἰ μὴ καλῶς
52 τι ποιοῦμεν, προτιθέντων ἡμῶν καὶ οὐκ ἀγρίως ἐπι-

ταττόντων ποιεῖν ἃ ἂν κελεύωμεν, ἀλλὰ ἐφιέντων δυοῖν
θάτερα, ἢ πείθειν ἡμᾶς ἢ ποιεῖν, τούτων οὐδέτερα ποιεῖ.

By remaining in Athens Socrates has tacitly accepted them;
he claimed, moreover, at his trial, that he preferred death to
banishment.

Ταύταις δή φαμεν καὶ σέ, ὦ Σώκρατες, ταῖς αἰτίαις
ἐνέξεσθαι, εἴπερ ποιήσεις ἃ ἐπινοεῖς, καὶ οὐχ ἥκιστα 5
Ἀθηναίων σέ, ἀλλ' ἐν τοῖς μάλιστα." εἰ οὖν ἐγὼ
εἴποιμι· " Διὰ τί δή;" ἴσως ἄν μου δικαίως καθάπτοιντο
λέγοντες ὅτι ἐν τοῖς μάλιστα Ἀθηναίων ἐγὼ αὐτοῖς
ὡμολογηκὼς τυγχάνω ταύτην τὴν ὁμολογίαν. φαῖεν
γὰρ ἂν ὅτι "Ὦ Σώκρατες, μεγάλα ἡμῖν τούτων Β
τεκμήριά ἐστιν, ὅτι σοι καὶ ἡμεῖς ἠρέσκομεν καὶ ἡ
πόλις· οὐ γὰρ ἄν ποτε τῶν ἄλλων Ἀθηναίων ἁπάντων
διαφερόντως ἐν αὐτῇ ἐπεδήμεις εἰ μή σοι διαφερόντως
ἤρεσκεν, καὶ οὔτ' ἐπὶ θεωρίαν πώποτ' ἐκ τῆς πόλεως 5
ἐξῆλθες, ὅτι μὴ ἅπαξ εἰς Ἰσθμόν, οὔτε ἄλλοσε οὐδαμόσε, εἰ μή ποι στρατευσόμενος, οὔτε ἄλλην ἀποδημίαν
ἐποιήσω πώποτε ὥσπερ οἱ ἄλλοι ἄνθρωποι, οὐδ' ἐπιθυμία
σε ἄλλης πόλεως οὐδὲ ἄλλων νόμων ἔλαβεν εἰδέναι,
ἀλλὰ ἡμεῖς σοι ἱκανοὶ ἦμεν καὶ ἡ ἡμετέρα πόλις· οὕτω 10
σφόδρα ἡμᾶς ᾑροῦ καὶ ὡμολόγεις καθ' ἡμᾶς πολιτεύ- C
σεσθαι, τά τε ἄλλα καὶ παῖδας ἐν αὐτῇ ἐποιήσω, ὡς
ἀρεσκούσης σοι τῆς πόλεως. ἔτι τοίνυν ἐν αὐτῇ τῇ δίκῃ
ἐξῆν σοι φυγῆς τιμήσασθαι εἰ ἐβούλου, καὶ ὅπερ νῦν
ἀκούσης τῆς πόλεως ἐπιχειρεῖς, τότε ἑκούσης ποιῆσαι. 5
σὺ δὲ τότε μὲν ἐκαλλωπίζου ὡς οὐκ ἀγανακτῶν εἰ δέοι
τεθνάναι σε, ἀλλὰ ᾑροῦ, ὡς ἔφησθα, πρὸ τῆς φυγῆς
θάνατον· νῦν δὲ οὔτ' ἐκείνους τοὺς λόγους αἰσχύνῃ,
οὔτε ἡμῶν τῶν νόμων ἐντρέπῃ, ἐπιχειρῶν διαφθεῖραι,
πράττεις τε ἅπερ ἂν δοῦλος ὁ φαυλότατος πράξειεν, D
ἀποδιδράσκειν ἐπιχειρῶν παρὰ τὰς συνθήκας τε καὶ τὰς
ὁμολογίας καθ' ἃς ἡμῖν συνέθου πολιτεύεσθαι. πρῶτον
μὲν οὖν ἡμῖν τοῦτ' αὐτὸ ἀπόκριναι, εἰ ἀληθῆ λέγομεν

5 φάσκοντές σε ὡμολογηκέναι πολιτεύσεσθαι καθ' ἡμᾶς
ἔργῳ ἀλλ' οὐ λόγῳ, ἢ οὐκ ἀληθῆ." τί φῶμεν πρὸς
ταῦτα, ὦ Κρίτων; ἄλλο τι ἢ ὁμολογῶμεν;
ΚΡ. Ἀνάγκη, ὦ Σώκρατες.

*He has never desired to live elsewhere: if he escapes, his
friends will suffer, and no well-governed state will receive him.*

Soc. Then will they not say: 'You, Socrates, are
10 breaking the covenants and agreements which you made
E with us at your leisure, not in any haste or under any
compulsion or deception, but after you have had seventy
years to think of them, during which time you were at
liberty to leave the city, if we were not to your mind,
5 or if our covenants appeared to you to be unfair.   You
had your choice, and might have gone either to Lacedaemon or Crete, both of which states are often praised
by you for their good government, or to some other
53 Hellenic or foreign state.   Whereas you, above all
other Athenians, seemed to be so fond of the state,
or, in other words, of us her laws (and who would care
about a state which has no laws ?), that you never stirred
5 out of her; the halt, the blind, the maimed were not
more stationary in her than you were.   And now you
run away and forsake your agreements.   Not so,
Socrates, if you will take our advice ; do not make
yourself ridiculous by escaping out of the city.
10   'For just consider, if you transgress and err in this
sort of way, what good will you do either to yourself
B or to your friends ?   That your friends will be driven
into exile and deprived of citizenship, or will lose their
property, is tolerably certain ; and you yourself, if you
fly to one of the neighbouring cities, as, for example,
5 Thebes or Megara, both of which are well governed,
will come to them as an enemy, Socrates, and their
government will be against you, and all patriotic citizens
will cast an evil eye upon you as a subverter of the laws,
and you will confirm in the minds of the judges the
c justice of their own condemnation of you.   For he who
is a corrupter of the laws is more than likely to be
a corrupter of the young and foolish portion of mankind.

Will you then flee from well-ordered cities and virtuous
men ? and is existence worth having on these terms ? 5
Or will you go to them without shame, and talk to
them, Socrates ? And what will you say to them ?
What you say here about virtue and justice and institutions and laws being the best things among men ?
Would that be decent of you ? Surely not. D

*If he goes to ill-governed Thessaly, his life will be nothing
but degradation. He need feel no anxiety for his children,
whose welfare is assured.*

'But if you go away from well-governed states to Crito's
friends in Thessaly, where there is great disorder and
licence, they will be charmed to hear the tale of your
escape from prison, set off with ludicrous particulars of 5
the manner in which you were wrapped in a goatskin
or some other disguise, and metamorphosed as the
manner is of runaways; but will there be no one to
remind you that in your old age you were not ashamed
to violate the most sacred laws from a miserable desire E
of a little more life ? Perhaps not, if you keep them
in a good temper; but if they are out of temper you
will hear many degrading things; you will live, but
how ?—as the flatterer of all men, and the servant of 5
all men; and doing what ?—eating and drinking in
Thessaly, having gone abroad in order that you may
get a dinner. And where will be your fine sentiments
about justice and virtue ? Say that you wish to live 54
for the sake of your children—you want to bring them
up and educate them—will you take them into Thessaly
and deprive them of Athenian citizenship ? Is this
the benefit which you will confer upon them ? Or are 5
you under the impression that they will be better cared
for and educated here if you are still alive, although
absent from them ; for your friends will take care of
them ? Do you fancy that if you are an inhabitant of
Thessaly they will take care of them, and if you are an 10
inhabitant of the other world that they will not take care
of them ? Nay; but if they who call themselves friends
are good for anything, they will—to be sure they will. B

He must face the laws of the next world with a clear conscience. Escape therefore is not permissible, and the voice of God must be obeyed.

"Ἀλλ', ὦ Σώκρατες, πειθόμενος ἡμῖν τοῖς σοῖς τροφεῦσι μήτε παῖδας περὶ πλείονος ποιοῦ μήτε τὸ ζῆν μήτε ἄλλο μηδὲν πρὸ τοῦ δικαίου, ἵνα εἰς Ἅιδου ἐλθὼν 5 ἔχῃς πάντα ταῦτα ἀπολογήσασθαι τοῖς ἐκεῖ ἄρχουσιν· οὔτε γὰρ ἐνθάδε σοι φαίνεται ταῦτα πράττοντι ἄμεινον εἶναι οὐδὲ δικαιότερον οὐδὲ ὁσιώτερον, οὐδὲ ἄλλῳ τῶν σῶν οὐδενί, οὔτε ἐκεῖσε ἀφικομένῳ ἄμεινον ἔσται. ἀλλὰ νῦν μὲν ἠδικημένος ἄπει, ἐὰν ἀπίῃς, οὐχ ὑφ' ἡμῶν τῶν c νόμων ἀλλὰ ὑπ' ἀνθρώπων· ἐὰν δὲ ἐξέλθῃς οὕτως αἰσχρῶς ἀνταδικήσας τε καὶ ἀντικακουργήσας, τὰς σαυτοῦ ὁμολογίας τε καὶ συνθήκας τὰς πρὸς ἡμᾶς παραβὰς καὶ κακὰ ἐργασάμενος τούτους οὓς ἥκιστα 5 ἔδει, σαυτόν τε καὶ φίλους καὶ πατρίδα καὶ ἡμᾶς, ἡμεῖς τέ σοι χαλεπανοῦμεν ζῶντι, καὶ ἐκεῖ οἱ ἡμέτεροι ἀδελφοὶ οἱ ἐν Ἅιδου νόμοι οὐκ εὐμενῶς σε ὑποδέξονται, εἰδότες ὅτι καὶ ἡμᾶς ἐπεχείρησας ἀπολέσαι τὸ σὸν μέρος. ἀλλὰ μή σε πείσῃ Κρίτων ποιεῖν ἃ λέγει μᾶλλον D ἢ ἡμεῖς."

Ταῦτα, ὦ φίλε ἑταῖρε Κρίτων, εὖ ἴσθι ὅτι ἐγὼ δοκῶ ἀκούειν, ὥσπερ οἱ κορυβαντιῶντες τῶν αὐλῶν δοκοῦσιν ἀκούειν, καὶ ἐν ἐμοὶ αὕτη ἡ ἠχὴ τούτων τῶν λόγων 5 βομβεῖ καὶ ποιεῖ μὴ δύνασθαι τῶν ἄλλων ἀκούειν· ἀλλὰ ἴσθι, ὅσα γε τὰ νῦν ἐμοὶ δοκοῦντα, ἐὰν λέγῃς παρὰ ταῦτα, μάτην ἐρεῖς. ὅμως μέντοι εἴ τι οἴει πλέον ποιήσειν, λέγε.

ΚΡ. Ἀλλ', ὦ Σώκρατες, οὐκ ἔχω λέγειν.

E   ΣΩ. Ἔα τοίνυν, ὦ Κρίτων, καὶ πράττωμεν ταύτῃ, ἐπειδὴ ταύτῃ ὁ θεὸς ὑφηγεῖται.

SCENE III. THE LAST DAY

Echecrates of Phlius asks Phaedo, who was present in the prison when Socrates was put to death, to tell the story of his last hours.

Ech. WERE you yourself, Phaedo, in the prison with 57 Socrates on the day when he drank the poison?

Phaed. Yes, Echecrates, I was.

Ech. I should so like to hear about his death. What did he say in his last hours? We were informed that 5 he died by taking poison, but no one knew anything more; for no Phliasian ever goes to Athens now, and it is a long time since any stranger from Athens has B found his way hither; so that we had no clear account.

Phaed. Did you not hear of the proceedings at the 58 trial?

Ech. Yes; some one told us about the trial, and we could not understand why, having been condemned, he should have been put to death, not at the time, but long 5 afterwards. What was the reason of this?

Phaedo tells of the delay in executing the sentence, and of the Delian mission-ship.

ΦΑΙΔ. Τύχη τις αὐτῷ, ὦ 'Εχέκρατες, συνέβη· ἔτυχεν γὰρ τῇ προτεραίᾳ τῆς δίκης ἡ πρύμνα ἐστεμμένη τοῦ πλοίου ὃ εἰς Δῆλον 'Αθηναῖοι πέμπουσιν.

ΕΧ. Τοῦτο δὲ δὴ τί ἐστιν;   10

ΦΑΙΔ. Τοῦτ' ἔστι τὸ πλοῖον, ὥς φασιν 'Αθηναῖοι, ἐν ᾧ Θησεύς ποτε εἰς Κρήτην τοὺς "δὶς ἑπτὰ" ἐκείνους ᾤχετο ἄγων καὶ ἔσωσέ τε καὶ αὐτὸς ἐσώθη. τῷ οὖν B 'Απόλλωνι ηὔξαντο ὡς λέγεται τότε, εἰ σωθεῖεν, ἑκάστου ἔτους θεωρίαν ἀπάξειν εἰς Δῆλον· ἣν δὴ ἀεὶ καὶ νῦν ἔτι ἐξ ἐκείνου κατ' ἐνιαυτὸν τῷ θεῷ πέμπουσιν. ἐπειδὰν οὖν ἄρξωνται τῆς θεωρίας, νόμος ἐστὶν αὐτοῖς ἐν τῷ χρόνῳ 5 τούτῳ καθαρεύειν τὴν πόλιν καὶ δημοσίᾳ μηδένα ἀποκτεινύναι, πρὶν ἂν εἰς Δῆλόν τε ἀφίκηται τὸ πλοῖον καὶ πάλιν δεῦρο· τοῦτο δ' ἐνίοτε ἐν πολλῷ χρόνῳ γίγνεται,

c ὅταν τύχωσιν ἄνεμοι ἀπολαβόντες αὐτούς. ἀρχὴ δ'
ἐστὶ τῆς θεωρίας ἐπειδὰν ὁ ἱερεὺς τοῦ Ἀπόλλωνος
στέψῃ τὴν πρύμναν τοῦ πλοίου· τοῦτο δ' ἔτυχεν,
ὥσπερ λέγω, τῇ προτεραίᾳ τῆς δίκης γεγονός. διὰ
5 ταῦτα καὶ πολὺς χρόνος ἐγένετο τῷ Σωκράτει ἐν τῷ
δεσμωτηρίῳ ὁ μεταξὺ τῆς δίκης τε καὶ τοῦ θανάτου.

*He describes the effect of the scene upon himself and the other
companions of Socrates, and recalls the names of those who were
present.*

Ech. What was the manner of his death, Phaedo?
What was said or done? And which of his friends
were with him? Or did the authorities forbid them to
10 be present—so that he had no friends near him when
he died?

d *Phaed.* No; there were several of them with him.

Ech. If you have nothing to do, I wish that you
would tell me what passed, as exactly as you can.

Phaed. I have nothing at all to do, and will try
5 to gratify your wish. To be reminded of Socrates is
always the greatest delight to me, whether I speak
myself or hear another speak of him.

Ech. You will have listeners who are of the same
mind with you, and I hope that you will be as exact as
10 you can.

e *Phaed.* I had a singular feeling at being in his
company. For I could hardly believe that I was present
at the death of a friend, and therefore I did not pity
him, Echecrates; he died so fearlessly, and his words
5 and bearing were so noble and gracious, that to me
he appeared blessed. I thought that in going to the
other world he could not be without a divine call, and
59 that he would be happy, if any man ever was, when he
arrived there; and therefore I did not pity him as might
have seemed natural at such an hour. But I had not
the pleasure which I usually feel in philosophical dis-
5 course (for philosophy was the theme of which we
spoke). I was pleased, but in the pleasure there was
also a strange admixture of pain; for I reflected that he
was soon to die, and this double feeling was shared
by us all; we were laughing and weeping by turns,

especially the excitable Apollodorus—you know the B
sort of man?

Ech. Yes.

Phaed. He was quite beside himself; and I and all
of us were greatly moved.   5

Ech. Who were present?

Phaed. Of native Athenians there were, besides
Apollodorus, Critobulus and his father Crito, Hermo-
genes, Epigenes, Aeschines, Antisthenes; likewise
Ctesippus of the deme of Paeania, Menexenus, and 10
some others; Plato, if I am not mistaken, was ill.

Ech. Were there any strangers?   c

Phaed. Yes, there were: Simmias the Theban, and
Cebes and Phaedondes; Euclid and Terpsion, who
came from Megara.

Ech. And was Aristippus there, and Cleombrotus?   5

Phaed. No, they were said to be in Aegina.

Ech. Any one else?

Phaed. I think that these were nearly all.

Ech. Well, and what did you talk about?

*How his friends gathered together, and were admitted to the
prison. The grief of Xanthippe.*

ΦΑΙΔ. Ἐγώ σοι ἐξ ἀρχῆς πάντα πειράσομαι διη- 10
γήσασθαι. ἀεὶ γὰρ δὴ καὶ τὰς πρόσθεν ἡμέρας D
εἰώθεμεν φοιτᾶν καὶ ἐγὼ καὶ οἱ ἄλλοι παρὰ τὸν
Σωκράτη, συλλεγόμενοι ἕωθεν εἰς τὸ δικαστήριον ἐν
ᾧ καὶ ἡ δίκη ἐγένετο· πλησίον γὰρ ἦν τοῦ δεσμωτηρίου. περιεμένομεν οὖν ἑκάστοτε ἕως ἀνοιχθείη τὸ 5
δεσμωτήριον, διατρίβοντες μετ' ἀλλήλων, ἀνεῴγετο
γὰρ οὐ πρῴ· ἐπειδὴ δὲ ἀνοιχθείη, εἰσῇμεν παρὰ τὸν
Σωκράτη καὶ τὰ πολλὰ διημερεύομεν μετ' αὐτοῦ. καὶ
δὴ καὶ τότε πρωαίτερον συνελέγημεν· τῇ γὰρ προτεραίᾳ
ἡμέρᾳ ἐπειδὴ ἐξήλθομεν ἐκ τοῦ δεσμωτηρίου ἑσπέρας, E
ἐπυθόμεθα ὅτι τὸ πλοῖον ἐκ Δήλου ἀφιγμένον εἴη.
παρηγγείλαμεν οὖν ἀλλήλοις ἥκειν ὡς πρωαίτατα εἰς
τὸ εἰωθός. καὶ ἥκομεν καὶ ἡμῖν ἐξελθὼν ὁ θυρωρός,
ὅσπερ εἰώθει ὑπακούειν, εἶπεν περιμένειν καὶ μὴ πρό- 5
τερον παριέναι ἕως ἂν αὐτὸς κελεύσῃ. "Λύουσι γάρ",

ἔφη, " οἱ ἕνδεκα Σωκράτη καὶ παραγγέλλουσιν ὅπως
ἂν τῇδε τῇ ἡμέρᾳ τελευτᾷ." οὐ πολὺν δ' οὖν χρόνον
ἐπισχὼν ἧκεν καὶ ἐκέλευεν ἡμᾶς εἰσιέναι. εἰσιόντες
60 οὖν κατελαμβάνομεν τὸν μὲν Σωκράτη ἄρτι λελυμένον,
τὴν δὲ Ξανθίππην—γιγνώσκεις γάρ—ἔχουσάν τε τὸ
παιδίον αὐτοῦ καὶ παρακαθημένην. ὡς οὖν εἶδεν ἡμᾶς
ἡ Ξανθίππη, ἀνηυφήμησέ τε καὶ τοιαῦτ' ἄττα εἶπεν, οἷα
5 δὴ εἰώθασιν αἱ γυναῖκες, ὅτι " Ὦ Σώκρατες, ὕστατον
δή σε προσεροῦσι νῦν οἱ ἐπιτήδειοι καὶ σὺ τούτους." καὶ
ὁ Σωκράτης βλέψας εἰς τὸν Κρίτωνα, " Ὦ Κρίτων,"
ἔφη, " ἀπαγέτω τις αὐτὴν οἴκαδε."

*Socrates, released from his bonds, speaks of pleasure and
pain.*

Some of Crito's people accordingly led her away,
B crying out and beating herself. And when she was
gone, Socrates, sitting up on the couch, bent and rubbed
his leg, saying, as he was rubbing: How singular is the
thing called pleasure, and how curiously related to pain,
5 which might be thought to be the opposite of it ; for they
are never present to a man at the same instant, and yet
he who pursues either is generally compelled to take
the other ; their bodies are two, but they are joined by
c a single head. And I cannot help thinking that if
Aesop had remembered them, he would have made
a fable about God trying to reconcile their strife, and
how, when he could not, he fastened their heads together ;
5 and this is the reason why when one comes the other
follows : as I know by my own experience now, when
after the pain in my leg which was caused by the chain,
pleasure appears to succeed.

. . . . .

*After this Socrates converses with his friends upon philosophy
as a purification and preparation for death, and upon the im-
mortality of the soul, whose lot in the future life is determined
by the nature of its conduct while upon the earth. He concludes
that a man who has striven in his lifetime to follow virtue need
never fear death. For himself, his time has come.*

114 c   Wherefore, Simmias, seeing all these things, what

ought not we to do that we may obtain virtue and
wisdom in this life? Fair is the prize, and the hope
great!

A man of sense ought not to say, nor will I be very D
confident, that the description which I have given of
the soul and her mansions is exactly true. But I do
say that, inasmuch as the soul is shown to be immortal,
he may venture to think, not improperly or unworthily, 5
that something of the kind is true. The venture is
a glorious one, and he ought to comfort himself with
words like these,, which is the reason why I lengthen
out the tale. Wherefore, I say, let a man be of good
cheer about his soul, who having cast away the pleasures E
and ornaments of the body as alien to him and working
harm rather than good, has sought after the pleasures
of knowledge ; and has arrayed the soul, not in some
foreign attire, but in her own proper jewels, temperance, 5
and justice, and courage, and nobility, and truth—in 115
these adorned she is ready to go on her journey to the
world below, when her hour comes. You, Simmias and
Cebes, and all other men, will depart at some time
or other. Me already, as a tragic poet would say, the 5
voice of fate calls. Soon I must drink the poison ; and
I think that I had better repair to the bath first, in order
that the women may not have the trouble of washing my
body after I am dead.

*The charge of Socrates to his friends, to follow in his footsteps.
The manner of his burial is immaterial : the true Socrates will
be far away.*

Ταῦτα δὴ εἰπόντος αὐτοῦ ὁ Κρίτων, Εἶεν, ἔφη, B
ὦ Σώκρατες· τί δὲ τούτοις ἢ ἐμοὶ ἐπιστέλλεις ἢ περὶ
τῶν παίδων ἢ περὶ ἄλλου του, ὅτι ἄν σοι ποιοῦντες
ἡμεῖς ἐν χάριτι μάλιστα ποιοῖμεν;

Ἅπερ ἀεὶ λέγω, ἔφη, ὦ Κρίτων, οὐδὲν καινότερον· 5
ὅτι ὑμῶν αὐτῶν ἐπιμελούμενοι ὑμεῖς καὶ ἐμοὶ καὶ τοῖς
ἐμοῖς καὶ ὑμῖν αὐτοῖς ἐν χάριτι ποιήσετε ἅττ᾽ ἂν ποιῆτε,
κἂν μὴ νῦν ὁμολογήσητε· ἐὰν δὲ ὑμῶν μὲν αὐτῶν
ἀμελῆτε καὶ μὴ ᾽θέλητε ὥσπερ κατ᾽ ἴχνη κατὰ τὰ νῦν
τε εἰρημένα καὶ τὰ ἐν τῷ ἔμπροσθεν χρόνῳ ζῆν, οὐδὲ 10

ἐὰν πολλὰ ὁμολογήσητε ἐν τῷ παρόντι καὶ σφόδρα,
c οὐδὲν πλέον ποιήσετε.
   Ταῦτα μὲν τοίνυν προθυμησόμεθα, ἔφη, οὕτω ποιεῖν.
θάπτωμεν δέ σε τίνα τρόπον;
   "Ὅπως ἄν, ἔφη, βούλησθε, ἐάνπερ γε λάβητέ με καὶ
5 μὴ ἐκφύγω ὑμᾶς. Γελάσας δὲ ἅμα ἡσυχῇ καὶ πρὸς
ἡμᾶς ἀποβλέψας εἶπεν· Οὐ πείθω, ὦ ἄνδρες, Κρίτωνα,
ὡς ἐγώ εἰμι οὗτος Σωκράτης, ὁ νυνὶ διαλεγόμενος καὶ
διατάττων ἕκαστον τῶν λεγομένων, ἀλλ᾽ οἴεταί με
ἐκεῖνον εἶναι ὃν ὄψεται ὀλίγον ὕστερον νεκρόν, καὶ
D ἐρωτᾷ δὴ πῶς με θάπτῃ.   ὅτι δὲ ἐγὼ πάλαι πολὺν
λόγον πεποίημαι, ὡς, ἐπειδὰν πίω τὸ φάρμακον, οὐκέτι
ὑμῖν παραμενῶ, ἀλλ᾽ οἰχήσομαι ἀπιὼν εἰς μακάρων δή
τινας εὐδαιμονίας, ταῦτά μοι δοκῶ αὐτῷ ἄλλως λέγειν,
5 παραμυθούμενος ἅμα μὲν ὑμᾶς, ἅμα δ᾽ ἐμαυτόν.

*He comforts Crito. After bathing, he converses with his
children and the women, and dismisses them.*

   And therefore I want you to be surety for me to
him now, as at the trial he was surety to the judges
for me : but let the promise be of another sort ; for he
was surety for me to the judges that I would remain,
10 and you must be my surety to him that I shall not
E remain, but go away and depart ; and then he will suffer
less at my death, and not be grieved when he sees my
body being burned or buried.   I would not have him
sorrow at my hard lot, or say at the burial, Thus we
5 lay out Socrates, or, Thus we follow him to the grave
or bury him ; for false words are not only evil in themselves, but they infect the soul with evil.   Be of good
cheer then, my dear Crito, and say that you are burying
116 my body only, and do with that whatever is usual, and
what you think best.
   When he had spoken these words, he arose and went
into a chamber to bathe ; Crito followed him, and told
5 us to wait.   So we remained behind, talking and thinking of the subject of discourse, and also of the greatness
of our sorrow ; he was like a father of whom we were
being bereaved, and we were about to pass the rest of

our lives as orphans. When he had taken the bath his B
children were brought to him (he had two young sons
and an elder one); and the women of the family also
came, and he talked to them and gave them a few directions in the presence of Crito; then he dismissed them 5
and returned to us.

*Just before sunset, the executioner arrives to tell Socrates that
he must die.*

Καὶ ἦν ἤδη ἐγγὺς ἡλίου δυσμῶν· χρόνον γὰρ πολὺν
διέτριψεν ἔνδον. ἐλθὼν δ᾽ ἐκαθέζετο λελουμένος καὶ
οὐ πολλὰ ἄττα μετὰ ταῦτα διελέχθη, καὶ ἦκεν ὁ τῶν
ἕνδεκα ὑπηρέτης καὶ στὰς παρ᾽ αὐτόν, Ὦ Σώκρατες, C
ἔφη, οὐ καταγνώσομαί γε σοῦ ὅπερ ἄλλων καταγιγνώσκω, ὅτι μοι χαλεπαίνουσι καὶ καταρῶνται ἐπειδὰν
αὐτοῖς παραγγείλω πίνειν τὸ φάρμακον ἀναγκαζόντων
τῶν ἀρχόντων. σὲ δὲ ἐγὼ καὶ ἄλλως ἔγνωκα ἐν τούτῳ 5
τῷ χρόνῳ γενναιότατον καὶ πρᾳότατον καὶ ἄριστον
ἄνδρα ὄντα τῶν πώποτε δεῦρο ἀφικομένων, καὶ δὴ καὶ
νῦν εὖ οἶδ᾽ ὅτι οὐκ ἐμοὶ χαλεπαίνεις, γιγνώσκεις γὰρ
τοὺς αἰτίους, ἀλλὰ ἐκείνοις. νῦν οὖν, οἶσθα γὰρ ἃ ἦλθον
ἀγγέλλων, χαῖρέ τε καὶ πειρῶ ὡς ῥᾷστα φέρειν τὰ D
ἀναγκαῖα. Καὶ ἅμα δακρύσας μεταστρεφόμενος ἀπῄει.

Καὶ ὁ Σωκράτης ἀναβλέψας πρὸς αὐτόν, Καὶ σύ,
ἔφη, χαῖρε, καὶ ἡμεῖς ταῦτα ποιήσομεν. Καὶ ἅμα πρὸς
ἡμᾶς, Ὡς ἀστεῖος, ἔφη, ὁ ἄνθρωπος· καὶ παρὰ πάντα 5
μοι τὸν χρόνον προσῄει καὶ διελέγετο ἐνίοτε καὶ ἦν
ἀνδρῶν λῷστος, καὶ νῦν ὡς γενναίως με ἀποδακρύει.
ἀλλ᾽ ἄγε δή, ὦ Κρίτων, πειθώμεθα αὐτῷ, καὶ ἐνεγκάτω
τις τὸ φάρμακον, εἰ τέτριπται· εἰ δὲ μή, τριψάτω
ὁ ἄνθρωπος.   10

Crito unsuccessfully urges him to delay. The last prayer.

Yet, said Crito, the sun is still upon the hill-tops, E
and I know that many a one has taken the draught late,
and after the announcement has been made to him, he
has eaten and drunk, and enjoyed the society of his
beloved; do not hurry—there is time enough.

Socrates said: Yes, Crito, and they of whom you speak are right in so acting, for they think that they will be gainers by the delay; but I am right in not
117 following their example, for I do not think that I should gain anything by drinking the poison a little later; I should only be ridiculous in my own eyes for sparing and saving a life which is already forfeit. Please then
5 to do as I say, and not to refuse me.

Crito made a sign to the servant, who was standing by; and he went out, and having been absent for some time, returned with the jailer carrying the cup of poison. Socrates said: You, my good friend, who are experi-
10 enced in these matters, shall give me directions how I am to proceed. The man answered: You have only
B to walk about until your legs are heavy, and then to lie down, and the poison will act. At the same time he handed the cup to Socrates, who in the easiest and gen- tlest manner, without the least fear or change of colour
5 or feature, looking at the man with all his eyes, Eche- crates, as his manner was, took the cup and said : What do you say about making a libation out of this cup to any god? May I, or not? The man answered: We only prepare, Socrates, just so much as we deem enough.
C I understand, he said : but I may and must ask the gods to prosper my journey from this to the other world— even so—and so be it according to my prayer.

The sorrow of his friends. The effect of the hemlock. Last words.

Καὶ ἅμ' εἰπὼν ταῦτα ἐπισχόμενος καὶ μάλα εὐχερῶς
5 καὶ εὐκόλως ἐξέπιεν. καὶ ἡμῶν οἱ πολλοὶ τέως μὲν ἐπιεικῶς οἷοί τε ἦσαν κατέχειν τὸ μὴ δακρύειν, ὡς δὲ εἴδομεν πίνοντά τε καὶ πεπωκότα, οὐκέτι, ἀλλ' ἐμοῦ γε βίᾳ καὶ αὐτοῦ ἀστακτὶ ἐχώρει τὰ δάκρυα, ὥστε ἐγκα- λυψάμενος ἀπέκλαον ἐμαυτόν—οὐ γὰρ δὴ ἐκεῖνόν γε,
D ἀλλὰ τὴν ἐμαυτοῦ τύχην, οἵου ἀνδρὸς ἑταίρου ἐστερη- μένος εἴην. ὁ δὲ Κρίτων ἔτι πρότερος ἐμοῦ, ἐπειδὴ οὐχ οἷός τ' ἦν κατέχειν τὰ δάκρυα, ἐξανέστη. Ἀπολλό- δωρος δὲ καὶ ἐν τῷ ἔμπροσθεν χρόνῳ οὐδὲν ἐπαύετο
5 δακρύων, καὶ δὴ καὶ τότε ἀναβρυχησάμενος κλάων καὶ

ἀγανακτῶν οὐδένα ὄντινα οὐ κατέκλασε τῶν παρόντων
πλήν γε αὐτοῦ Σωκράτους.

Ἐκεῖνος δέ, Οἷα, ἔφη, ποιεῖτε, ὦ θαυμάσιοι. ἐγὼ
μέντοι οὐχ ἥκιστα τούτου ἕνεκα τὰς γυναῖκας ἀπέπεμψα,
ἵνα μὴ τοιαῦτα πλημμελοῖεν· καὶ γὰρ ἀκήκοα ὅτι ἐν Ε
εὐφημίᾳ χρὴ τελευτᾶν. ἀλλ' ἡσυχίαν τε ἄγετε καὶ
καρτερεῖτε.

Καὶ ἡμεῖς ἀκούσαντες ᾐσχύνθημέν τε καὶ ἐπέσχομεν
τοῦ δακρύειν. ὁ δὲ περιελθών, ἐπειδή οἱ βαρύνεσθαι 5
ἔφη τὰ σκέλη, κατεκλίνη ὕπτιος—οὕτω γὰρ ἐκέλευεν
ὁ ἄνθρωπος—καὶ ἅμα ἐφαπτόμενος αὐτοῦ οὗτος ὁ δοὺς
τὸ φάρμακον, διαλιπὼν χρόνον ἐπεσκόπει τοὺς πόδας
καὶ τὰ σκέλη, κἄπειτα σφόδρα πιέσας αὐτοῦ τὸν πόδα
ἤρετο εἰ αἰσθάνοιτο, ὁ δ' οὐκ ἔφη. καὶ μετὰ τοῦτο 10
αὖθις τὰς κνήμας· καὶ ἐπανιὼν οὕτως ἡμῖν ἐπεδείκνυτο 118
ὅτι ψύχοιτό τε καὶ πήγνυτο. καὶ αὐτὸς ἥπτετο καὶ
εἶπεν ὅτι, ἐπειδὰν πρὸς τῇ καρδίᾳ γένηται αὐτῷ, τότε
οἰχήσεται.

Ἤδη οὖν σχεδόν τι αὐτοῦ ἦν τὰ περὶ τὸ ἦτρον 5
ψυχόμενα, καὶ ἐκκαλυψάμενος—ἐνεκεκάλυπτο γάρ—
εἶπεν—ὃ δὴ τελευταῖον ἐφθέγξατο—Ὦ Κρίτων, ἔφη,
τῷ Ἀσκληπιῷ ὀφείλομεν ἀλεκτρυόνα· ἀλλὰ ἀπόδοτε
καὶ μὴ ἀμελήσητε.

Ἀλλὰ ταῦτα, ἔφη, ἔσται, ὁ Κρίτων· ἀλλ' ὅρα εἴ τι 10
ἄλλο λέγεις.

Ταῦτα ἐρομένου αὐτοῦ οὐδὲν ἔτι ἀπεκρίνατο, ἀλλ'
ὀλίγον χρόνον διαλιπὼν ἐκινήθη τε καὶ ὁ ἄνθρωπος
ἐξεκάλυψεν αὐτόν, καὶ ὃς τὰ ὄμματα ἔστησεν· ἰδὼν
δὲ ὁ Κρίτων συνέλαβε τὸ στόμα καὶ τοὺς ὀφθαλμούς. 15

Ἥδε ἡ τελευτή, ὦ Ἐχέκρατες, τοῦ ἑταίρου ἡμῖν
ἐγένετο, ἀνδρός, ὡς ἡμεῖς φαῖμεν ἄν, τῶν τότε ὧν
ἐπειράθημεν ἀρίστου καὶ ἄλλως φρονιμωτάτου καὶ
δικαιοτάτου.

NOTES

I. THE APOLOGY

17 A. The case for the prosecution is closed, and Socrates comes forward to the speakers' platform (βῆμα) to reply. His opening words are a reproof of the professional pleader, who sacrifices truth for the sake of effect. Plato, whose artistic instinct is unerring, makes him speak throughout in a homely, simple fashion, though his very earnestness makes him rise to great heights of eloquence.

17 B 9. ἤ τι ἤ οὐδέν, 'little or nothing of the truth'.

17 B 11–C 1. κεκαλλιεπημένους . . . ὀνόμασιν. The sophist-trained speakers spent much time in mastering the technique of oratory. Such speeches would never contain 'things spoken at random in the words which come handy at the moment'.

17 C 4. τῇδε τῇ ἡλικίᾳ, 'for me at my age'. He was now, as he tells us later, seventy years old. His statement does not strike us as remarkable, but the Athenian was never averse from litigation ; his experience as a juryman, or visits to the courts out of curiosity, would make the procedure thoroughly familiar—he would be no ξένος there.

17 C 9. ἐπὶ τῶν τραπεζῶν. The bankers and money-changers chose the market-place for their tables or counters, because all men passed that way. So too we find them in the New Testament transacting business in the temple-courts at the Passover.

17 D 1. θορυβεῖν. A warning which Socrates has occasion to repeat. The formal solemnity of an English court would make the Greek counterpart appear to us as disorderly as a mass-meeting.

17 D 2–3. πρῶτον. If he has escaped the ordeal so long, it should prove how harmless his way of life has been hitherto. ἀναβαίνω is used of mounting the speakers' platform, or of 'coming up to the court'.

17 D 4. τῆς ἐνθάδε λέξεως. Aristophanes in the *Clouds* depicts Strepsiades as going to Socrates for the very purpose of learning this kind of oratory.

17 D 5. συνεγιγνώσκετε. From the time of Pericles onward, Athens was full of foreigners, who were recognized as a valuable asset to the state, and treated with consideration.

18 A 2–3. δίκαιον, ὥς γέ μοι δοκῶ: parenthetical; 'a piece of justice, in my opinion'.

18 A 3–4. ἴσως μὲν . . . εἴη. He has no doubt that it is better, but such εἰρωνεία is characteristic. εἰρωνεία is 'understatement', and so 'ignorance falsely assumed'.

18 A 6. ῥήτορος δί. Many of his audience would have preferred to say that the virtue of an orator is to be πιθανός 'convincing '.

18 A 8. older charges : for these see Introd. p. 15.

18 B 2. during many years. The *Clouds* had appeared twenty-four years before. Perhaps those who saw it at the time are now beginning to wonder whether 'there may have been something in it after all '.

18 B 8-9. the heaven above . . . the earth beneath. The inquiries of scientists into the nature of the universe have always been so regarded ; compare the case of Galileo.

18 B 9-10. made the worse appear the better cause. The *Clouds* shows that the sophists had a reputation for teaching men to argue black white ; compare the claim of Protagoras to teach them how to make the weaker argument prevail.

18 C 8. went by default. Socrates never defended himself until now because he felt that his whole life was an adequate refutation.

19 B 4-5. an affidavit. This summarizes the criticisms of Aristophanes.   **a curious person,** i. e. a busybody, a meddler. The comedian Eupolis pokes fun at him as πτωχὸν ἀδολέσχην 'a beggarly gossip '.

19 C 4-5. walks in air. In the *Clouds* Socrates is discovered in his 'school', slung up in a basket, in order to prevent the attraction of the earth from hindering the ethereal nature of his thoughts.

19 C 11. physical speculations. Socrates turned from these at an early age, being more interested in the relation of man to the world than in the nature of the world itself, in the question ' why ? ' than in the question ' how ? '.

19 D 9. οὐδέ γε : more emphatic than a second οὔτε.

19 E 1. πράττομαι. Socrates felt that by expecting a fee, a teacher was making himself the slave of his pupil, and although Aristophanes implies that he charged for his teaching, there is no doubt that he was mistaken.   **ἐπεί.** Possibly there is an ellipse here, e. g. ' I don't find fault with such people, for . . .'.

19 E 3-4. Γοργίας . . . Πρόδικος . . . Ἱππίας : for these, and the whole class of professional teachers or sophists, see Introd. p. 9.

20 A 1. τὰς ἐκείνων συνουσίας. One of the objections felt by older men to the sophists was that they were often foreigners, claiming to give the young men a better education than their own country-men could. Notice how the parenthesis leads to an alteration in the construction of this sentence.

20 A 8. πώλω ἢ μόσχω. An analogy like this always appealed to Socrates ; the oriental mind would probably employ a parable.

20 B 1. τὴν προσήκουσαν ἀρετήν : cognate acc., ' in their appropriate virtue '. It is explained below as ἀνθρωπίνη τε καὶ πολιτική, the virtue of a man and a citizen.

20 B 7-8. Τίς . . . ποδαπός . . . πόσου. The eagerness of Socrates to find such a man is shown by his rapid questions, and the confidence of Callias by his concise answers. It is impossible to mistake the good-natured irony with which Evenus and his claims are summed up.

20 B 9. πέντε μνῶν, i.e. all the knowledge a man could want in return for a couple of £10 notes!

20 C 3. ἀλλ' οὐ γάρ is emphatic : 'but indeed I don't . . .'.

20 E 6. something extravagant. The Gk. μέγα λέγειν is as direct as the American phrase, 'to talk big'. This characteristic of directness in both languages may be frequently noticed.

21 A 1. Chaerephon : a devoted friend and follower of Socrates, and a butt for the comic poets, who made fun of his dark, sallow complexion, and accused him of many things for which there was probably slight foundation. In the *Clouds* he is spoken of as helping his master to calculate how many of its own feet a flea could jump.

21 A 2. recent exile, i.e. four years before, during the rule of the Thirty Tyrants. Their policy of wholesale confiscation of property and of killing or banishing their political opponents lasted only 8 months, after which the popular party under Thrasybulus returned in strength and restored the democracy.

21 A 8. the Pythian prophetess. Her replies were given in a trance, under the supposed influence of the god. Her words on this occasion have been recorded :

σοφὸς Σοφοκλῆς, σοφώτερος Εὐριπίδης
ἀνδρῶν δ' ἁπάντων Σωκράτης σοφώτατος.

21 B 7. he is a god, and cannot lie. There is a good deal of irony in this account ; if the god cannot lie, it is impiety to try to disprove his words. Socrates continually criticizes the Olympian gods on the score of immorality, though for Apollo he had the greatest respect, and makes him the official god of his ideal 'Republic'. But Apollo had a world-wide reputation, and Delphi was far more than the shrine of a tribal or national god.

21 C 7. a politician. Athenians thought highly of their politicians, who would naturally be the first people to attract the attention of a man who was searching for wisdom at Athens.

21 E 6. τὸ τοῦ θεοῦ, sc. πρᾶγμα, 'the business of the god'.

21 E 7. τὸν χρησμὸν τί λέγει, 'the meaning of the oracle', a more vigorous way of saying ὅ τι λέγοι ὁ χρησμός.

21 E 9-22 A 1. νὴ τὸν κύνα. The oath which avoids profanity, present in almost every language.

22 A 3. ὀλίγου δεῖν κτλ., 'to be almost the most deficient'; τοῦ belongs to εἶναι, the whole phrase being dependent on ὀλίγου δεῖν.

22 A 7. πόνους . . . πονοῦντος, sc. ἐμοῦ. He speaks as if he were Hercules come to life again.

22 A 9. τοὺς ποιητάς. The following passage exemplifies the interest taken by Socrates in poets and craftsmen, to whom he continually turns throughout his conversations for analogies and illustrations.

22 B 1. διθυράμβων. Probably this refers to lyric poetry in general.

22 B 4. μάλιστα πεπραγματεῦσθαι, 'to be most polished'. The classic example in English poetry is Gray's 'Elegy', on which he is said to have spent two or three years.   **διηρώτων ἄν:** iterative *ἄν*, denoting customary action.

22 B 7. ὀλίγου αὐτῶν ἅπαντες, 'almost all of them'.

22 C 1-2. φύσει τινὶ καὶ ἐνθουσιάζοντες. Inspiration is always regarded as the truest source of poetry, though we perhaps should not compare it, as Socrates does here, to the divinely inspired frenzy of the dervish.

22 C 4-5. πάθος . . . πεπονθότες, 'to experience something like this'.

22 C 6-7. σοφωτάτων εἶναι ἀνθρώπων. Notice this rather colloquial form of attraction, where the accusative case might normally be expected.

22 D 3. τούτου μέν is followed here not by *δέ*, but by the more emphatic *ἀλλά*.

22 D 9. ἀποκρύπτειν, sc. *ἔδοξε*, supplied from *ἔδοξαν* in 22 D 5.

22 E 1-2. πότερα δεξαίμην ἄν κτλ., 'whether I would rather be as I am'.

23 A 4. the wisdom . . . wanting in others. Socrates is always at pains to make it clear that he is only a seeker, and not a possessor, of wisdom: it is not difficult to see why this was only regarded as sarcasm.

23 B 3. And so I go about, &c.: a clear statement of his mission, his method, and the consequences.

23 B 9. public matters of interest always absorbed the Athenians, and a man who took no interest in them was *ἰδιώτης* a 'mugwump'.

23 D 1. The indignation of these people is so essentially human and true to life that it is not difficult to sympathize with them; perhaps it is not too much to suppose that Socrates did too in his heart, though never admitting it.

23 E 1. numerous. The vast majority would not have understood his views in the least.

23 E 5-6. Μέλητος . . . Ἄνυτος . . . Λύκων: see Introd. p. 16.

24 A 1-2. ὅπερ ἀρχόμενος ἐγὼ ἔλεγον: see 19 A.

24 A 6. ὑποστειλάμενος: an obvious metaphor to a nation of seamen; from taking in sail, and so 'drawing back' or 'shrinking'.

24 A 7. αὐτοῖς τούτοις, 'for these same reasons'.

24 B 5. τὸν ἀγαθὸν καὶ φιλόπολιν, ὥς φησι. Probably this is exactly what he did say; the irony of the last two words is almost audible as we read them.

24 B 7. ὥσπερ ἑτέρων . . . κατηγόρων, 'as if these were a second set of accusers', though in reality they have nothing fresh to add. So Socrates continues: 'It runs somewhat as follows', describing the charges rather vaguely and placing them in the wrong order.

24 C 1. δαιμόνια, 'spiritual' or 'supernatural beings': perhaps the indictment aims at the δαιμόνιον or 'voice', of which Socrates speaks later.

24 C 5. Μέλητον. The position is emphatic, and is echoed by ἐμέλησεν in 24 C 8, probably an intentional pun.

24 C 10. The cross-examination which follows is a characteristic example of the 'dialectic' method. It is amusing to see Meletus forced to answer of sheer necessity, in order to save his face, and to mark how by every fresh question he is drawn a little nearer to his doom.

25 A 12. The conclusion, though it is not actually stated, is again drawn from horse-training ; Socrates appeals to the sense of the judges to infer the rest of the analogy, and leaves us to picture the angry confusion of Meletus.

25 C 6. The second series of questions is equally damaging to Meletus, though it would not carry much weight as a piece of apologetics.

26 A 1-3. The claim that if he offends unintentionally, he ought to be privately instructed, shows that Socrates attaches far more importance to motives than to consequences. How far ought we to agree with him in this?

26 B 1. οὔτε μέγα οὔτε μικρόν, 'neither much nor little', both accusatives being adverbial.

26 B 4-5. θεοὺς . . . μὴ νομίζειν. The whole phrase follows something like διαφθείρειν με φῂς τοὺς νεωτέρους, understood from the last sentence.

26 B 5. οὓς ἡ πόλις νομίζει : an accurate expression, for the traditional religion was essentially a state religion and an external one.

26 B 6. ταῦτα : obj. of διδάσκων, but emphatic in position.

26 C 1-7. This is really a simple sentence comprising a double indirect question ; the emphasis in the first part is on τινάς, explained and elaborated by the parenthesis and the following relative clause. Notice how Socrates insists on having his points absolutely clear before he begins to deal with them.

26 C 8. τὸ παράπαν οὐ νομίζεις θεούς. Aristophanes implies as much in the *Clouds* when he makes Socrates say in one place : 'The gods don't pass current among us'.

26 D 6. 'Αναξαγόρου. Anaxagoras was an Ionian philosopher from Clazomenae who spent much of his time at Athens. He was a friend of Pericles and Euripides, the former of whom saved him from death when he was accused of impiety.

26 D 7. οὕτω is to be taken both with καταφρονεῖς and ἀπείρους. τῶνδε refers to the jury.

26 D 9. καὶ δὴ καί κτλ., 'and what is more, the young men learn this from me, when they can buy it at times for a drachma at the most in the orchestra, and make fun of Socrates if he claims them as his own theories'. This implies one of two things : (a) the orchestra of the theatre of Dionysius at Athens was used as a book-stall when no performance was on ; (b) there was some other spot in Athens so used and known as the ὀρχήστρα.

26 E 6-7. Ἄπιστος . . . σαυτῷ: because, as he will now show, Anytus does not allow that Socrates believes in any gods, and yet accuses him of teaching the young men to believe in δαιμόνια καινά, which are surely a kind of gods.

26 E 10—27 A 1. ὥσπερ αἴνιγμα συντιθέντι, sc. τινί, 'like a man who is composing a riddle'. διαπειρωμένῳ is in apposition and introduces the question.

27 A 2. ὁ σοφὸς δή. The particle is intensely ironical.

27 A 7. παίζοντος, 'the part of a man who is jesting'. Cp. the gen. in phrases like *hominis est errare.*

27 B 2. my accustomed manner, i.e. of catechizing a man into self-contradiction! No wonder he warns the audience not to make an outcry. Meletus himself will hardly answer, so surely does he know the fate which awaits him.

27 B 7-8. horsemanship . . . flute-playing: the common things of everyday life once again.

28 B 2. At this point the defence proper closes, and the next passage is a digression, in which Socrates defends the whole tenor of his life. His text might well have been : ' What shall it profit a man if he gain the whole world and lose his own soul ?'

28 C 2. son of Thetis. Achilles, the Greek champion, was a hero or demigod, as being the son of Thetis and Peleus. The slaying of Trojan Hector at his hands is the culminating tragedy of the *Iliad.*

28 D 7-8. ὑπ' ἄρχοντος: here the commander in the field, and not the civil magistrate.

28 D 10–E 1. δεινὰ ἂν εἴην εἰργασμένος κτλ. The structure of this sentence is a little difficult ; in outline it is as follows : ' I should have done a terrible thing if, when military commanders posted me, I remained at my post, but ran away when under God's orders to live in a certain manner.' It is this inconsistency which is δεινόν.

28 E 6. δεῖν is really superfluous, and only repeats the force of τάττοντος one line above. Athenian armies were operating at Potidaea from 432 to 430 B. C. The battle of Amphipolis, at which Brasidas and Cleon were both killed, took place in 422 B. C., two years after the Athenian defeat at Delium. Alcibiades describes Socrates during the retreat from Delium as 'stalking like a pelican, and rolling his eyes, making very intelligible to anybody, even from a distance, that whoever attacked him would be likely to meet with a stout resistance ' (*Symposium* 221).

29 A 1. εἰσάγοι, 'might hale me into court'.

29 A 2-3. ἀπειθῶν . . . δεδιώς . . . οἰόμενος. The participles are an explanation of ὅτι οὐ νομίζω θεοὺς εἶναι.

29 A 6. τὸν θάνατον : taken out of its clause as subj. of τυγχάνει and joined to the principal verb as object, a common idiom both in Latin and Greek. τῷ ἀνθρώπῳ, 'to mankind'.

29 B 3. τούτῳ, 'in this respect', strengthened by the addition of καὶ ἐνταῦθα.

29 B 5. τῷ ... του, 'than any man in any respect', the Greek order being the reverse of the English. τούτῳ ἄν, sc. φαίην σοφώτερος εἶναι.

29 B 7. τὸ δὲ ἀδικεῖν ... οἶδα. Notice the emphasis which is obtained by the unusual order of words in this sentence. The whole is nothing more than his way of saying: 'No man can serve two masters'.

29 B 12. There is a striking parallel to the following passage in the reply of the Apostles to the Sanhedrim in Acts v.

29 D 3. I honour and love you. It is interesting to see how irrepressibly Socrates' sense of humour forces its way to the surface, even when he is approaching the most serious part of his defence.

29 E 2-3. improvement of the soul. The Socratic conception of the soul was essentially novel, and must have puzzled the average Athenian very much.

30 A 4. citizen and alien, &c. Compare St. Paul's 'First the Jew, then the Gentile'.

30 A 5-6. the command of God. He is speaking now with the sincerest conviction about his divinely appointed mission, and is met by another outbreak of disorder.

30 C 2-3. ἐμμείνατέ μοι, 'please abide by'.

30 C 5. ἄττα ... καὶ ἄλλα, 'some other things too'.

30 C 7-8. οὐκ ἐμὲ μείζω κτλ. This is characteristic Greek understatement, and means, of course, 'You will harm yourselves far more than me'.

30 D 1. δύναιτο: to be taken with both Μέλητος and Ἄνυτος.

30 D 2-3. ἀποκτείνειε ... ἐξελάσειεν ... ἀτιμώσειεν: the three heaviest forms of punishment which could be inflicted.

30 D 9-E 1. ἐμοῦ καταψηφισάμενοι, 'by condemning me'.

30 E 2. γελοιότερον. This simile, for which he apologizes, is one of the most famous of all his sayings.

30 E 3. ὑπὸ τοῦ θεοῦ: with προσκείμενον, which serves as a passive of προστίθημι.

30 E 5. οἶον δή, 'in which capacity in fact'.

30 E 7-8. ἕνα ἕκαστον: with the preceding ὑμᾶς.

31 A 1. προσκαθίζων returns to the gadfly metaphor: 'settling upon'.

31 A 3. ἴσως τάχ' ἄν: a strengthened form of ἴσως. The five particles which follow provide a good exercise in translation.

31 C 4. my poverty. The Athenians were not singular in thinking that a man must be enthusiastic, not to say a little mad, if he is ready to endure poverty, when it is avoidable. 'The fear of poverty in the upper classes to-day is the greatest barrier to moral progress.'—William James.

31 D 4. it always forbids but never commands. Xenophon tells us that Socrates did receive positive commands in this way, and turned the gift to his own and his friends' advantage, but Plato's version is the more probable one. Perhaps the 'voice' was a strong negative intuition.

31 E 3. the truth is, &c. We can see clearly from this passage that Socrates was no democrat, and distrusted the governing powers of the multitude. In his ideal state supreme power is in the hands of the philosopher-king ; here he implies that a successful politician at Athens must necessarily be dishonest.

32 A 5. λόγους . . . ἔργα. The Athenians may have thought that they preferred 'deeds', not words', but in reality they resembled most democracies in being at the mercy of any brilliant speaker. Compare Cleon's speech about Sphacteria (Thucydides iv) with some of our modern election addresses.

32 A 6. οὐδ' ἂν ἑνί: far more emphatic than οὐδενὶ ἄν.

32 A 8. δικανικά. It was customary for the accused to produce evidence of good service to the state, as well as of his virtues in private life ; such evidence might well be 'boring'.

32 B 1. ἐβούλευσα δέ, 'but I was a member of the Council'.

32 B 2. Ἀντιοχίς: probably the marginal note of a scribe, which found its way into the text.   **πρυτανεύουσα.** The βουλή was made up of 500 members, taken in equal numbers from each of the ten tribes. Each group of fifty acted as an executive committee (πρυτάνεις) for the rest for one-tenth of the year (πρυτανεία). The committee, which presided over the ἐκκλησία if it were summoned, sat in the θόλος, or 'round chamber', mentioned below, under a chairman elected for the day (ἐπιστάτης).

32 B 3. τοὺς δέκα στρατηγούς. After the naval victory of the Athenians at Arginusae in 406 B. C., at which, as a fact, only eight of the generals were present, the dead and wounded had not been picked up owing to the sudden rising of a storm. Popular indignation was stirred up against the generals, and it was proposed that they should be tried as a body, and put to death if found guilty. The unlawful character of the proposal lies in the fact that they could legally claim to be tried separately ; furthermore, they did not receive a fair hearing.

32 B 5. ἐν τῷ ὑστέρῳ χρόνῳ : very shortly afterwards, though the ringleaders of the agitation escaped before their trial came on.

32 B 7. ἐναντία ἐψηφισάμην. According to Xenophon, Socrates was chairman on this occasion, and it was his business to put the question to the vote. It appears therefore (a) either that he voted in committee against the proposal that the question should be put to the assembly, and that this and the preceding clause are reversed in actual order of occurrence ; (b) or that the Committee fell out about the putting of the question after the assembly had been summoned. In any case his experience in a public capacity was sufficiently exciting, and the whole story throws a strong light on the declining years of Athenian democracy.

32 B 8. ἀπάγειν, 'to have me arrested on the spot'. These ῥήτορες are professional demagogues.

32 C 4. ὀλιγαρχία : see Introd. p. 8.

32 C 6. Λέοντα. We only know that he was an able and honest man.

32 D 1. ἀναπλῆσαι, lit. 'to infect ', and so 'involve in '.

32 D 2-3 εἰ μὴ ἀγροικότερον ἦν εἰπεῖν, 'were it not rather a blunt thing to say'. Yet he says it, and leaves the jury to infer what his estimation of them is.   οὐδ' ὁτιοῦν, 'not a rap'.

32 D 4. τούτου δέ sums up the previous phrase, δέ repeating the δέ of the last line.

32 D 9. διὰ ταχέων κατελύθη. The Thirty maintained their position for eight months only. It has been suggested that Socrates was protected from them by his former pupil Critias.

32 E 2-6. Socrates is supremely careless of what his words imply with regard to the principles of the rest of the Athenians, and is clearly carried away by his earnestness.

33 A 4. my disciples, i.e. paying pupils. Those who followed him were merely associates on the usual terms of friendship or acquaintance. It appears possible, however, that Socrates may have received voluntary contributions to enable him to exist.

33 B 4. professed to teach. The sophists were literally *professors* of learning, who sometimes made the most extravagant claims for their systems of education.

33 C 4. there is amusement in it. We can almost see his covert smile, as he thinks of all the conventional Athenians who have been discomfited.

33 C 6-7. oracles, visions, &c. We have had an instance of the importance he attached to oracles already; an example of attention to a vision occurs during his conversation with Crito in prison.

33 D 8. Many of them. Of the associates mentioned below, Crito appears in the dialogue named after him. Aeschines was a prominent disciple of Socrates, who was present at his death; he seems to have been an unpractical person, and in later life became first a seller of perfumes and then a bankrupt. Plato was at this time twenty-four years old: it is significant of his habit of self-effacement that he is mentioned only in two other places in the dialogues. The rest of those named are unimportant.

34 A 7. make way for him. The allotted time for the speaker is measured by a water-clock; Socrates offers to sacrifice part of it to his opponents.

34 C 2-3. prayed and entreated the judges, &c. This was the prevalent fashion both in the Greek and in the Roman courts. A modern caricature of the method may be studied in the famous Bardell v. Pickwick trial in Dickens.

34 D 4. 'of wood or stone': quoted from *Od.* xix. 163. Whenever Socrates quotes Homer, it must be remembered that the *Iliad* and the *Odyssey* were to the Greeks very much what the Authorized Version is to us.

34 D 5-6. sons ... three in number. The name of the eldest was Lamprocles, those of the other two were Sophroniscus and Menexenus.

35 A 2. διαφέρειν, 'to be superior'.

35 A 3. τοιοῦτοι, i.e. the sort of people who indulge in these appeals to the emotions.

35 A 6-7. πείσεσθαι: fut. inf. of πάσχω.   ἀθανάτων ἐσομένων. The gen. abs. adds emphatic irony, where we might have expected an acc. case, in agreement with αὐτούς.

35 B 1. περιάπτειν. The metaphor is from putting on a garment. ὥστ' ἄν . . . ὑπολαβεῖν, instead of a potential optat., 'so that any stranger might suppose '.

35 B 8. τοῦ . . . εἰσάγοντος, 'the man who introduces these moving stage-effects'.

35 C 2. διδάσκειν καὶ πείθειν. Socrates has ideals of justice which correspond to all the rest of his views ; therefore he assumes a jury of intelligent and impartial persons, who have nothing but a sense of duty before them.

35 C 6. ἐθίζεσθαι, 'to let yourselves be accustomed '.

35 C 7. εὐσεβοῖεν. It is curious, in view of the charge of impiety, to learn what he thinks is entailed by an oath ; he would have been interested in the modern view of perjury.   ἀξιοῦτε, 'expect'.

35 D 2. ἄλλως τε belong to καί, the words between being inserted rather violently in order to strengthen his affirmation.

35 D 7. νομίζω τε γάρ, sc. θεούς, 'I believe in them, as do none of my accusers'. The quiet note of his closing sentence is a good instance of Greek restraint and directness.

. . . .

36 A. With reference to this second speech, we may note the difference between the ἀγὼν ἀτίμητος, where the penalty is fixed by law, and the ἀγὼν τιμητός, where, after the verdict, the penalty is assessed by the jury, after speeches in which both the prosecution and the defence propose what they consider to be a suitable penalty. Meletus has proposed death ; Socrates has to propose a counter-penalty. For one or other of these the jury must vote.

36 A 4-5. the majority against me. Apparently 281 votes were cast against him, the minority vote being 220. By adding 31 to the latter—Socrates is speaking in round numbers—we get 251 for and 250 against.

36 A 10. a fifth part, i.e. 281 votes altogether amount in jest to 93⅔ for each of the three accusers: but Socrates is ironical, when he subdivides them thus. The fine of a thousand drachmae was paid into the public funds, the idea being to discourage frivolous litigation.

36 B 7. to be idle. The offices and occupations mentioned below are little better than idleness to Socrates, though the many despised a man who did not devote his whole life to them.

36 B 9-10. speaking in the assembly. For a specimen of the activities of the professional orators see 32 B.   plots (in Gk. συνωμοσίαι): the political clubs of Athens. According to Thucydides, party-strife (στάσις) was the most disruptive influence in the Greek states during the last half of the fifth century.

36 C 1-2. too honest . . . to be a politician. Even if we feel as he does about politics, this is not the most practical way of obtaining clean government.

36 D 8. **Prytaneum**: the town-hall, used for the entertainment of ambassadors, state guests, victors in the games, and pensioners. He is only half-serious in saying this, of course, but his defiant spirit is magnificent.

36 E 2–3. **appearance ... reality.** This contrast contains the germ of Socrates' view that the ultimate realities of life are to be found in the realm of thought, and that the concrete phenomena of experience are merely reflections of them; this in brief is his Theory of Ideas, which was afterwards developed by Plato.

37 A 9. **in other cities.** Perhaps this refers to Sparta, whose constitution Socrates frequently praised; if so, his boldness is marvellous, when we consider how fresh the memory of the war was in the minds of his hearers.

37 C 2. **the Eleven**: the Athenian commissioners of police, one from each tribe, with an additional member as secretary.

37 C 7–8. τιμήσωμαι ... τιμήσαιτε. Notice the gen. case after these two verbs.

37 D 5. ζῆν is explanatory, to be taken with καλὸς ... ὁ βίος, 'a fine life it would be for me to live'.

37 E 3. Σιγῶν δέ κτλ. Socrates puts the question into the mouths of his audience so as to get yet another opportunity for affirming his earnestness with regard to his mission.

38 A 3–6. ἑκάστης ἡμέρας ... ἐξεταζόντος. This long phrase explains τοῦτο and is in effect the subject of τυγχάνει. ὁ δὲ ἀνεξέταστος βίος. In this famous phrase we have his whole attitude summed up.

38 A 7–8. τὰ δὲ ἔχει μὲν οὕτως. Notice the demonstrative use of the article, which is not uncommon in colloquial Greek.

38 B 2. οὐδὲν γὰρ ἂν ἐβλάβην. Loss of money is no evil, so that he is still consistent in what he has already laid down about not deserving anything evil.

38 B 5. μνᾶν ἀργυρίου. This small sum is not named ironically, for he probably could not afford to pay much more. His whole estate when he died amounted to only 5 minae, or about £20.

      .   .   .   .

38 C. The prevailing note of this final speech is one of extraordinary dignity, and as a piece of composition is one of Plato's finest achievements.

38 D 3–4. It is perfectly clear throughout that Socrates is not concerned to procure his acquittal at all, but only to 'bear witness of the truth'. It has been said that his defence amounts almost to suicide.

39 B 8–9. **let them abide by theirs.** There can have been few among his hearers so biased as not to feel some pangs of conscience at these words. Socrates is not far from the truth when he says it is fated; yet the Jews who crucified Christ were free agents and responsible.

39 C I. τὸ δὲ δὴ μετὰ τοῦτο, 'but next'.   χρησμῳδῆσαι: as Jacob does in the book of Genesis, and Hector and Patroclus in the *Iliad*.

39 C 6. ἢ οἵαν ἐμὲ ἀπεκτόνατε, 'than the punishment of death which you have inflicted on me': sc. τιμωρίαν, a cognate acc. extending the sense of the verb.

39 D 1. πλείους ἔσονται. Schools of philosophy sprang up in which his theories were developed, but none of his successors performed the same function of μύωψ to Athens.

39 D 4-5. ἀποκτείνοντες . . . ἐπισχήσειν. The truth of his statement is amply proved by the history of religious persecution in all ages.

39 E 3. the magistrates. This refers to the Eleven, and not to the nine archons.

40 A and B. In speaking thus Socrates is only half-serious, and is adjusting his ideas to the level of his audience. It is improbable that he would have consoled himself in the face of death by such a consideration; his belief that death is not an evil is rooted far deeper. Xenophon tells us that he was so fearless of the consequences that he refused to allow any one to draw up a set speech for his defence.

40 D 9. the great king, i. e. of Persia. Kings are always supposed to be within easier reach of happiness than ordinary men in accordance with the fallacy that happiness can be purchased at a price.

40 E 4-5. the journey to another place. Greek ideas of the next world were as shadowy as its occupants were supposed to be, save only among the followers of Orphism. It is difficult to believe, as we read this passage, that Socrates did not believe in a future life, though he does not state his views here in nearly such a concrete form as he does in the *Phaedo*. In that case, however, he was addressing a circle of intimate friends.

41 A 3-4. Of the judges mentioned, Rhadamanthus judges the souls of Asiatics, Aeacus those of Europeans, while Minos is president over a kind of final court of appeal (*Gorgias* 524 A). This is the only mention of Triptolemus in such a capacity, though he had a reputation as a lawgiver.

41 A 7. The names of Orpheus and Musaeus are both associated with the mysteries, and books attributed to them circulated freely in Athens at this time; according to legend they were both poets with supernatural powers of expression.

41 C 1. Odysseus or Sisyphus: both these are types of subtlety and deep knowledge.

41 C 9–D 1. ἕν τι τοῦτο . . . ἀληθές, 'this one thing as true'.

41 D 5. ἀπηλλάχθαι πραγμάτων, 'to be quit of the affairs of life'. On his last day of life Socrates spoke of the soul as being freed by death from the hindrance of the body.

41 D 8. οὐ πάνυ χαλεπαίνω. The force of οὐ πάνυ is either 'not at all', or, more commonly, 'scarcely'. If Socrates was in any degree angry, it is difficult to suppose him so for any other reason except their wilful blindness.

42 A 2. ἀλλὰ γάρ κτλ. 'But now it is time'. The quiet note of satisfaction on which he closes is a fitting conclusion to his conduct throughout the trial, and a fine example of Plato's art. We are left with a feeling that at this moment, if never before, the whole court is hushed and attentive.

II. THE CRITO

43 A 9. εὐεργέτηται. No doubt Crito had 'tipped' him handsomely, for the prison doors were not usually opened so early, as we learn later.

43 A 11. ἐπιεικῶς πάλαι, 'fairly long ago'.

43 B 3–4. οὐδ' ἂν αὐτὸς ἤθελον, 'I only wish that I were not', &c.

43 B 5. πάλαι θαυμάζω. Note the tense: Greek, Latin, and French all employ the present in such phrases.

43 B 6–7. ὡς ἥδιστα διάγῃς. Perhaps Crito is recalling the words of Socrates at his trial about death being annihilation. The tense shows that he expects him to sleep again presently.

43 C 8. ἐν τοῖς βαρύτατα κτλ., 'which perhaps I should find it hardest to bear'. ἐν τοῖς is probably an example of the pronominal use of the article, 'among them'; cf. πρὸ τοῦ. Ultimately it came to be merely a way of emphasizing the superlative.

43 C 9. τίνα ταύτην; sc. ἀγγελίαν φέρεις. πλοῖον. See *Phaedo* 58 A–C for a full account of the mission-ship.

43 D 3–4. ἀπὸ Σουνίου. Sunium is the promontory which forms the south-east corner of Attica.

43 D 7. τύχῃ ἀγαθῇ, 'good luck to us', a common form of well-wishing.

44 A 5. τῆς ἐπιούσης ἡμέρας, 'during the coming day'. Note the case, and compare with ταύτης τῆς νυκτός two lines lower.

44 A 6. τῆς ἑτέρας, 'the next day', i.e. 'to-morrow'.

44 A 6–7. ἐνυπνίου. Socrates in his defence referred to his belief in visions (33 C).

44 B 2–3. ἤματι . . . ἵκοιο : *Iliad* ix. 363, where Achilles is inclined to leave the siege of Troy and return home to Phthia ; so Socrates regards his impending death as a home-coming.

44 B 8. escape. The reasons urged by Crito for the attempt are instructive, for they show that he is really out of touch with Socrates and his modes of thought, although he is his oldest friend.

44 E 5. the informers. The Gk. word συκοφάντης is said to mean a man who made his living by detecting and exposing cases of attempted exportation of figs at a time when it was forbidden by law. In classical times it means simply 'informers', a regular class at Athens like *delatores* under the early Roman emperors.

45 A 7. get you out of prison. Conditions in the state-prison must have been lax, for the actual details of escape are regarded throughout this scene as the least troublesome part of the business.

45 B 3. strangers, i.e. foreigners, not Athenians. Simmias and Cebes, both Thebans, both followers of the doctrines of Pythagoras, had been drawn to Athens by the influence of Socrates. They were both present at his death, and therefore must have been among the inner circle of his friends.

45 E 3-4. The trial need never have come on. Crito seems to imply that Socrates might have settled with his accusers out of court, or else have withdrawn from Athens before his trial.

46 A 5. Note how, as his argument progresses, Crito becomes more and more eager and insistent: we can imagine Socrates' face growing more and more immovable in proportion, though he cannot have been unsympathetic to his old friend.

46 B 2. εἰ μετά τινος ὀρθότητος εἴη, 'if it were actuated by a sense of justice'. He then proceeds to prove carefully and methodically that it is not.

46 B 5. τῶν ἐμῶν, sc. λόγων.

46 C 2. οὐ μή ... συγχωρήσω (aor. subj.): a usual form of emphatic denial for the future.

46 C 3. πλείω, with μορμολύττηται, 'scare us with bugbears more than ever'.

46 C 6. πῶς οὖν. Here Socrates settles down to serious argument; the passage that follows is a typical instance of his method of opening a discussion. He begins by submitting the statements of Crito to the dialectic process, clearing the ground of possible causes of misunderstanding as he goes.

46 D 3. ἄλλως ἕνεκα λόγου, 'idly, for the sake of talking'.

46 D 6. φανεῖται, i. e. ὁ λόγος.

46 D 8. ὑπὸ τῶν οἰομένων τὶ λέγειν, 'those who thought they had something to say', i. e. people worth hearing, not mere babblers.

46 E 3. ὅσα γε τἀνθρώπεια, 'in all human probability'.

47 A 1. παρακρούοι: probably a metaphor from music, 'to strike a wrong note', so 'to mislead'.

47 A 9. ναί: the ordinary Greek affirmative. Crito is in the grip of the Socratic machine at once: he has no alternative answer, and is forced slowly and inevitably into the position which he instinctively desires to avoid.

47 B 3-4. his physician or trainer. The two between them would aim at producing health, strength, and beauty. Athletics as a subject of conversation would appeal to any Athenian, since they were a nation of athletes, though with no taint of professionalism.

47 D 5. that principle, i. e. the soul according to the new Socratic doctrine.

48 A 6. he, the one man. Socrates does not attempt to find out who he is, but if any man of the time deserved to be so called, that man was himself.

48 B 1. that will clearly be the answer. Crito takes up the suggestion with pathetic eagerness, only to have his hopes dashed again.

48 B 10. these premisses, i. e. that we must consider only the opinion of the expert, and that the expert is the man who knows the good life.

48 C 8. with as little reason. This contempt for the general run of mankind is not altogether inconsistent with the true humility of Socrates, which springs from continual contemplation of the highest things.

48 D 7. From this point onward Crito's replies lose all their sting; he seems to know in his heart already that his case is hopeless.

49 A 3. Socrates has disposed of Crito's arguments, and now begins to present his own point of view, beginning with the principle that it is wrong to requite evil with evil, which clears the ground for the still nobler 'Love your enemies' of the Gospel.

49 B 8. Observe how Socrates persists in his point until he brings Crito from an unwilling οὐ φαίνεται and a reluctant δῆπου through ἀληθῆ λέγεις to the emphatic ἀλλ' ἐμμένω τε καὶ συνδοκεῖ μοι. His watchword in argument is 'Thorough'.

49 D 1. ὀλίγοις τισί. It is only from this time forward that we meet any other doctrine than that of 'an eye for an eye, and a tooth for a tooth'. Even Crito takes time before he consents to be classed with the 'few' who think otherwise.

49 D 3. οὐκ ἔστι κοινὴ βουλή, 'they have no common grounds for discussion'. The two points of view cannot be reconciled, although we might disagree with the καταφρονεῖν of Socrates, and prefer pity to 'scorn', according to the law of charity.

49 D 6. ἀρχώμεθα ἐντεῦθεν βουλευόμενοι, 'we are to take this as a first principle in our deliberations'. The local gen. abs. which follows explains ἐντεῦθεν: tr. 'that it is never right', &c.

49 D 9. τῆς ἀρχῆς, 'the starting-point of our discussion'.

50 A 9-10. the laws and the government. From here Socrates abandons the method of question and answer, and by this famous personification of the Laws devotes all his energy to making his own point of view clear to Crito.

50 B 7. rhetorician. His opinion of the class was not flattering. There is an allusion here to a custom whereby no law could be repealed at Athens until it had been defended by recognized advocates.

50 D 8-11. education . . . music . . . gymnastic. In Greek education μουσική covers all the intellectual side, and not only music; it is balanced by the physical side, γυμναστική, and the effect of the two is designed to produce *mens sana in corpore sano.*

50 E 3-4. our child and slave, i.e. in complete subjection to the head of the family, in which light the state is regarded. At Rome the *patria potestas* carried the right of life and death over the children.

50 E 8. to strike . . . your father. In the *Clouds* Pheidippides proposes that, as his father beat him out of kindness in his childhood, he shall beat his father for the same reason, since he is in his second childhood. There was nothing more atrocious to the ancients than this particular offence against the laws of *pietas.*

51 A 6. In this passage Plato makes it clear that, in his opinion, Socrates was a good citizen, in spite of anything his countrymen said or felt to the contrary.

51 C 8. εἰ ἡμεῖς ταῦτα ἀληθῆ λέγομεν, 'if this that we have said is true'.

51 D 2-3. τῷ ἐξουσίαν πεποιηκέναι, 'by having given permission'.

51 D 3-4. δοκιμασθῇ. On attaining the age of eighteen, every Athenian was formally enrolled in the register of his deme ; the next two years were occupied with military service, after which he attained to full citizen rights. The δοκιμασία τῶν ἐφήβων was a scrutiny or examination which every youth had to pass before enrolment.

51 D 5. ἐξεῖναι follows προαγορεύομεν, 'we proclaim that he may', &c.

51 D 8-9. εἰς ἀποικίαν ἰέναι, i.e. to go to one of the Athenian colonies.   μετοικεῖν means to go to another state altogether and live there as a resident alien.

51 E 1. ὃς δ' ἂν ὑμῶν κτλ. This sentence is long, but simple in structure, if taken a clause at a time; like many other long sentences in Plato it is thoroughly colloquial.

52 A 5. εἴπερ ποιήσεις, (emphatic) 'if you insist on doing'.

52 A 8. ἐν τοῖς μάλιστα : cp. note on 43 C 8.

52 B 5. ἐπὶ θεωρίαν : the spectacle of the great public games.

52 B 8. ὥσπερ οἱ ἄλλοι ἄνθρωποι. We may infer that many of the Athenians travelled a good deal, whether on business or for pleasure.

52 B 9. εἰδέναι : an afterthought, added to explain the preceding ἐπιθυμία.

52 C 2. τά τε ἄλλα καί, 'and besides'.

52 C 4. φυγῆς τιμήσασθαι. The conclusion is that if he had done so, he would have been allowed to go.

52 C 7. ὡς ἔφησθα : see 37 D.

52 E 6-7. Lacedaemon or Crete. Socrates approved of both because they aimed at the production of good, law-abiding citizens by means of a rather severe discipline, which in his eyes opened the road to the truest freedom.

53 D 3. Thessaly, where every kind of violence and disorder was rife.

53 D 6. wrapped in a goatskin. This was the ordinary dress of the Attic farm-labourer.

53 E 3. in a good temper . . . out of temper. Men living under such an uncertain government might be expected to display uncertain tempers.

53 E 6. eating and drinking. The Thessalian always had a reputation as a *bon-vivant*.

54 C 1. ὑπ' ἀνθρώπων. The best laws can be badly administered.

54 C 5. σαυτόν τε . . . ἡμᾶς explains τούτους οὓς ἥκιστα ἔδει.

54 D 3. οἱ κορυβαντιῶντες, 'the frenzied priests of Cybele'. A wild dance accompanied by equally wild music formed an important part of their worship.

54 D 7. μάτην ἐρεῖς. As the Corybantes heard only the sound of their own music, which had an almost mesmeric effect, so Socrates is deaf to any sound save the voice of God.

III. THE PHAEDO

57 A I. **Phaedo** was a native of Elis, who was taken prisoner in the war and became a slave at Athens. His freedom was purchased at the instance of Socrates, whose devoted pupil he became.

57 A 7. **no Phliasian.** Phlius was a town situated in the mountains between Argolis and Arcadia ; its inhabitants were Dorian in origin and allied with Sparta, and had long been acquainted with the doctrines of Pythagoras.

58 A 7–9. τύχη τις, 'a coincidence'. ἔτυχεν . . . ἐστεμμένη, 'had just been crowned'.

58 A 12. τοὺς "δὶς ἑπτά" ἐκείνους, 'the well-known "fourteen"'. This is a traditional name for the seven youths and seven maidens who were sent every ninth year by the Athenians to Minos, king of Crete, in accordance with the advice of Apollo. In exchange for this offering to the Minotaur of the famous labyrinth, Minos undertook not to attack Athenian territory. On the third occasion of their going, Theseus, the great hero of Athenian mythology, went with them, killed the monster, and, after escaping from the labyrinth with the aid of Ariadne's ball of thread, brought the intended victims safely back.

58 B 3. θεωρίαν, 'the sacred mission', sent annually to Delos, the birthplace of Apollo and one of the chief centres of his worship.

58 B 7–8. καὶ πάλιν δεῦρο, i.e. back to Athens.

58 B 8. ἐν πολλῷ χρόνῳ γίγνεται, 'takes a long time'.

59 B and C. Of the persons mentioned here we have met some already at the trial. Not much is known of the others. Antisthenes founded the school of philosophers known as Cynic. There is a story of Cleombrotus of Ambracia, who is perhaps the man mentioned here, which tells how, after reading the *Phaedo* through, he bade the sun farewell and hurled himself into the sea from a lofty wall, being convinced by what he had just read of the blessing of death as leading to a better life. We may compare the famous Cato Uticensis, who read the whole work through twice on the last night of his life, and at dawn fell upon his sword and died.

59 D 2–3. φοιτᾶν . . . παρὰ τὸν Σωκράτη, 'to visit Socrates regularly'.

59 D 6. διατρίβοντες μετ᾽ ἀλλήλων, 'whiling away our time', i.e. in conversation, since they were all disciples of Socrates, and many of them Athenians.

59 E 3–4. εἰς τὸ εἰωθός, 'to the accustomed spot'.

59 E 5. εἶπεν περιμένειν, 'told us to wait'.

60 A 2. Ξανθίππην. Xanthippe, according to tradition, was an extremely aggravating wife, though Plato tells us nothing to con-

firm it. In any case Socrates, being a philosopher, was better qualified than most men to be her husband.

60 A 8. ἀπαγέτω τις αὐτὴν οἴκαδε. This sounds perhaps as if Socrates had not much consideration for her, but she and her children had clearly been allowed to spend the previous night in his company, so that she would naturally need rest. She returns later to bid him a final farewell.

60 C 2. Aesop. Herodotus tells us that he was a slave at Samos at the time when Croesus was king of Lydia, in the middle of the sixth century. Stories of this type, of which Brer Rabbit is perhaps the modern counterpart, were current at Athens at this time, but probably not in written form.

. . . .

With reference to the discussion which follows, it is certain that many of the arguments employed belonged properly to Plato rather than to Socrates; with this we are not immediately concerned. The actual incidents related in our text are most probably historic: they certainly fit in with what we know of Socrates during his trial and imprisonment.

. . . .

115 B 4. ἐν χάριτι μάλιστα ποιοῖμεν, 'we might serve you best'.

115 C 1. οὐδὲν πλέον ποιήσετε, 'you will achieve nothing'.

115 C 6. ἀποβλέψας, 'looking earnestly at us', and away from everything else.

115 D 1. ὅτι δὲ ἐγώ κτλ. The clause which begins here and ends at εὐδαιμονίας, is summed up in the ταῦτα which follows. 'Though I have been explaining at great length that when I have drunk the poison, I shall be with you no longer, but shall go hence to the joys of the blessed which you know of, yet in saying all this', &c.

115 D 7. at the trial he was surety. Crito had clearly pledged himself that Socrates would appear at his trial.

115 E 7-8. Be of good cheer then. Socrates abounds in sympathy, and it is difficult to believe that these kindly words of comfort failed in their purpose.

116 B 4-5. gave them a few directions. He is amazingly quiet and business-like. Plato reproduces the atmosphere of peaceful confidence with great skill.

116 C 2. οὐ καταγνώσομαί γε σοῦ, 'I shall not pass judgement upon you as I do upon others'.

116 C 5-6. ἐν τούτῳ τῷ χρόνῳ. He had been in prison a month.

116 C 8. οὐκ ἐμοί: emphatic by position ('it is not with me', &c.), balanced by ἀλλὰ ἐκείνοις.

116 D 2. δακρύσας, 'bursting into tears'. From what we learn in the next paragraph, it is clear that he too had fallen under the spell of Socrates' personality.

117 B 7. making a libation. Perhaps he is thinking of the death of Theramenes, who in similar circumstances had drunk a toast in hemlock-juice to his deadliest enemy Critias.

117 C 4. ἐπισχόμενος, 'raising the cup to his lips'.

117 C 7-8. οὐκέτι, 'we were no longer able to do so'.   ἐμοῦ γε
βίᾳ καὶ αὐτοῦ, 'in spite of myself'.

117 D 1. οἴου ἀνδρός κτλ. explains τύχην, 'my misfortune in being robbed of such a friend'.

117 D 6. οὐδένα ὄντινα οὐ = πάντας.

118 A 2. πήγνυτο is, like ψύχοιτο, optative, but is a very rare form.

118 A 8. τῷ 'Ασκληπιῷ . . . ἀλεκτρυόνα. Those who had been miraculously healed in the temple of Aesculapius while in a trance, used to bring a cock as a thank-offering. Socrates apparently means that he is falling asleep now to awake in the next world healed of the disease of Life.

118 A 13. ἐκινήθη, 'he quivered'.

118 A 14. καὶ ὃς τὰ ὄμματα ἔστησεν, lit. 'he (Socrates) fixed his eyes'; tr. 'and his eyes grew set'.

VOCABULARY

ἁβρύνομαι, I give myself airs.
ἀγαθός, -ή, -όν, good.
ἀγανακτέω, I am vexed, displeased.
ἀγγελία, -ας, ἡ, news, message.
ἀγγέλλω, ἀγγελῶ, ἤγγειλα, I announce, report.
ἄγγελος, -ου, ὁ, messenger.
ἀγορά, -ᾶς, ἡ, market-place.
ἀγρίως, adv., harshly, fiercely.
ἄγροικος, -ον, boorish, rude.
ἀγρυπνία, -ας, ἡ, sleeplessness, watching.
ἄγω, ἄξω, ἤγαγον, I lead, bring.
ἀγών, -ῶνος, ὁ, struggle, contest, lawsuit.
ἀδελφός, -οῦ, ὁ, brother.
ἄδηλος, -ον, unknown, uncertain.
ἀδικέω, I do wrong, act unjustly, ill-treat.
ἄδικος, -ον, wrong, unjust.
ἀδίκως, adv., wrongly, unjustly.
ἀδύνατος, -ον, unable; τὸ ἀδύνατον, the impossible.
ἀεί, adv., always.
ἀθάνατος, -ον, immortal.
ἄθεος, -ον, denying the gods, atheistic.
Ἀθηναῖος, -α, -ον, Athenian.
ἀθρόος, -α, -ον, all at once.
Ἅιδης, -ου, ὁ, the god of the lower world, Hades; τὰ ἐν Ἅιδου, the lower world.
αἴνιγμα, -ατος, τό, riddle.
αἱρέω, αἱρήσω, εἷλον, I take; mid., αἱρέομαι, ἑλοῦμαι, εἱλόμην, I choose.
αἰσθάνομαι, αἰσθήσομαι, ᾐσθόμην, I perceive, learn.
αἰσχρός, -ά, -όν, shameful, disgraceful.
αἰσχύνη, -ης, ἡ, shame, disgrace.
αἰσχύνομαι, I am ashamed.

αἰτία, -ας, ἡ, cause, charge, accusation, blame.
αἴτιος, -α, -ον, causing, responsible for.
ἀκολασία, -ας, ἡ, intemperance, extravagance.
ἀκόλαστος, -ον, unbridled, intemperate.
ἀκούω, ἀκούσομαι, ἤκουσα, ἀκήκοα, I listen, hear.
ἀκροάομαι, I hear, listen to.
ἄκων, -ουσα, -ον, unwilling, involuntary.
ἀλεκτρυών, -όνος, ὁ, cock.
ἀλήθεια, -ας, ἡ, truth.
ἀληθής, -ές, true, real.
ἀληθῶς, adv., really, truly.
ἁλίσκομαι, ἁλώσομαι, ἑάλων, I am caught.
ἀλλά, conj., but.
ἀλλήλους, -ας, -α (no nom.), one another, each other.
ἄλλοθι, adv., elsewhere.
ἀλλοῖος, -α, -ον, of another sort, different; comp., ἀλλοιότερος, -α, -ον.
ἄλλος, -η, -ο, another, other; ἄλλῃ, adv., in another place, way.
ἄλλοσε, adv., to another place.
ἄλλως, adv., in another way, otherwise; ἄλλως τε καί, especially.
ἀλόγιστος, -ον, thoughtless, unreasoning.
ἅμα, adv., at once, at the same time.
ἀμαθής, -ές, unlearned, stupid.
ἀμαθία, -ας, ἡ, ignorance.
ἁμάρτημα, -ατος, τό, mistake, error.
ἀμείβομαι, I change.
ἀμείνων, -ον, better.

98 VOCABULARY

ἀμελέω, I am careless, neglect.
ἀμύνομαι, I defend myself, requite.
Ἀμφίπολις, -εως, ἡ, Amphipolis, a town in Thrace, on the Strymon.
ἀμφότερος, -α, -ον, both.
ἄν, conditional or indefinite particle: also = ἐάν.
ἀναβαίνω, -βήσομαι, -έβην, I go up, mount.
ἀναβλέπω, I look up, look back at.
ἀναβρυχάομαι, I cry aloud.
ἀναγκάζω, -άσω, I compel.
ἀναγκαῖος, -α, -ον, necessary.
ἀνάγκη, -ης, ἡ, necessity.
ἀναιρέομαι, -ελοῦμαι, -ειλόμην, I take up.
ἀναλαμβάνω, -λήψομαι, -έλαβον, I take up, resume.
Ἀναξαγόρας, -ου, ὁ, Anaxagoras.
ἀναπίμπλημι, -πλήσω, -έπλησα, I fill up, taint, involve.
ἀνδρεία, -ας, ἡ, courage.
ἀνέλεγκτος, -ον, irrefutable.
ἄνεμος, -ου, ὁ, wind.
ἀνεξέταστος, -ον, unexamined, without inquiry.
ἀνέρομαι, -ηρόμην, I ask, question.
ἀνευφημέω, I cry out.
ἀνήρ, ἀνδρός, ὁ, man.
ἀνθρώπειος, -α, -ον / ἀνθρώπινος, -η, -ον, belonging to man, befitting man, human.
ἄνθρωπος, -ου, ὁ, man, human being.
ἀνοίγνυμι, -οίξω, -έῳξα, I open.
ἀνόσιος, -α, -ον, impious, wicked.
ἀνταδικέω, I injure, do wrong in return.
ἀντιδράω, I retaliate, do in return.
ἀντικακουργέω, I injure in return.
Ἀντιοχίς, ἡ, the tribe Antiochis.
ἀντωμοσία, -ας, ἡ, statement upon oath, affidavit.
Ἄνυτος, -ου, ὁ, Anytus.
ἄξιος, -α, -ον, worthy.
ἀξιόχρεως, -ων, worth considering, sufficient.

ἀξιόω, I think worthy, think, expect, claim.
ἀπαγγέλλω, -αγγελῶ, -ήγγειλα, I report, announce, relate.
ἀπαγορεύω, I forbid.
ἀπάγω, -άξω, -ήγαγον, I lead away, take home.
ἀπαλλαγή, -ῆς, ἡ, deliverance, release.
ἀπαλλάσσω, I set free, release, escape, get rid of.
ἅπαξ, adv., once.
ἅπας, ἅπασα, ἅπαν, all, all together.
ἀπειθέω, I disobey.
ἄπειρος, -ον, inexperienced, ignorant.
ἀπελαύνω, -ελῶ, -ήλασα, I drive away, expel.
ἀπέρχομαι, ἄπειμι, -ῆλθον, I go away, depart.
ἀπεχθάνομαι, -εχθήσομαι, -ηχθόμην, I am hated.
ἄπιστος, -ον, untrustworthy.
ἀποβαίνω, -βήσομαι, -έβην, I depart ; of events, to result, turn out.
ἀποβλέπω, I gaze upon.
ἀποδακρύω, I lament, weep for.
ἀποδημία, -ας, ἡ, absence from home, going abroad.
ἀποδιδράσκω, -δράσομαι, -έδραν, I run away, escape.
ἀποδίδωμι, I restore, pay.
ἀποθνήσκω, -θανοῦμαι, -έθανον, -τέθνηκα, I die, am killed.
ἀποικία, -ας, ἡ, settlement, colony.
ἀποκλάω, -κλαύσομαι, I weep for, bewail.
ἀποκρίνομαι, I answer, reply.
ἀποκρύπτω, I hide, conceal.
ἀποκτείνω, -κτενῶ, -έκτεινα, I put to death, kill.
ἀπολαμβάνω, -λήψομαι, -έλαβον, I take back, receive, keep back.
ἀπολείπω, -λείψω, -έλιπον, I leave behind.
Ἀπολλόδωρος, -ου, ὁ, Apollodorus.

ἀπόλλυμι, -ολῶ, -ώλεσα, I kill, destroy.
Ἀπόλλων, -ωνος, ὁ, Apollo.
ἀπολογέομαι, I make a defence.
ἀπολογία, -ας, ἡ, defence.
ἀποπέμπω, I send away.
ἀποτρέπω, I turn aside.
ἀποφεύγω, -φεύξομαι, -έφυγον, I escape, am acquitted.
ἅπτομαι, ἅψομαι, ἡψάμην, I touch.
ἆρα, interrog. particle.
ἄρα, so then.
ἀργύριον, -ου, τό, silver, money.
ἀρέσκω, ἀρέσω, ἤρεσα, I please, satisfy.
ἀρετή, -ῆς, ἡ, virtue, goodness, excellence.
ἄριστος, -η, -ον, best, noblest.
ἄρτι, adv., just now.
ἀρχή, -ῆς, ἡ, beginning, first principle; power, rule, office or magistracy.
ἄρχω, I hold office, rule; mid., ἄρχομαι, I begin.
ἄρχων, -οντος, ὁ, archon, chief magistrate, officer.
ἀσέβεια, -ας, ἡ, irreverence, impiety.
Ἀσκληπιός, -οῦ, ὁ, Asclepius, the god of medicine.
ἀστακτί, adv., in floods.
ἀστεῖος, -α, -ον, courteous, polite.
ἀτεχνῶς, adv., without art, simply; ἀτεχνῶς ξένως ἔχω, I am an utter stranger.
ἀτιμόω, I dishonour, punish with loss of citizen rights.
ἄτοπος, -ον, strange, odd, absurd.
ἄττα = τινά.
αὖ
αὖθις } adv., again, further.
αὐλός, -οῦ, ὁ, flute.
αὔριον, adv., to-morrow.
αὐτόματος, -η, -ον, spontaneous, without cause, natural.
αὐτός, -ή, -όν (weak demonst.), self; he, she, it; ὁ αὐτός, the same.
αὐτόφωρος, -ον, caught in the act

of stealing; ἐπ' αὐτοφώρῳ, in the very act.
ἀφαίρεσις, -εως, ἡ, a taking away, deprivation.
ἀφικνέομαι, -ίξομαι, -ικόμην, I come, arrive.
ἀφίστημι, I remove; mid., ἀφίσταμαι, I withdraw from.
ἄφρων, -ον, senseless, foolish.
ἄχθομαι, ἀχθέσομαι, ἠχθέσθην, I am vexed, distressed.

βαθύς, βαθεῖα, βαθύ, deep; ὄρθρος βαθύς, early morning.
βαρύνω, I burden, torment; pass., am weary.
βαρύς, βαρεῖα, βαρύ, heavy, troublesome, grievous.
βελτίων, -ον, better; superl., βέλτιστος, -η, -ον.
βία, -ας, ἡ, strength, force, violence.
βιάζομαι, I force, exercise compulsion.
βιβλίον, -ου, τό, book.
βιώσομαι, see ζάω.
βιωτός, -ή, -όν, to be lived, worth living.
βλάπτω, I harm, injure.
βλέπω, I look, see.
βοάω, I shout.
βομβέω, I hum.
βούλευμα, -ατος, τό, plan, resolution.
βουλεύω, I take counsel, consider, determine; also I am a member of the Council.
βουλή, -ῆς, ἡ, will, plan, advice; also the Council of 500 at Athens.
βούλομαι, I wish.

γάρ, conj., for.
γε, enclitic particle, at least, anyhow.
γελάω, I laugh.
γελοῖος, -α, -ον, laughable, ridiculous.

γέμω, I am full of.
γενναῖος, -α, -ον, noble, high-born, thoroughbred.
γενναίως, adv., nobly.
γεννάω, I beget, produce.
γεννητής, -οῦ, ὁ, parent.
γεωργικός, -ή, -όν, rustic.
γέρων, -οντος, ὁ, old man.
γῆ, γῆς, ἡ, earth.
γίγνομαι, γενήσομαι, ἐγενόμην, γέγονα, I become.
γιγνώσκω, γνώσομαι, ἔγνων, I learn, find out, know.
Γοργίας, -ου, ὁ, Gorgias, the famous sophist and rhetorician.
γοῦν, at any rate.
γράμμα, -ατος, τό, letter; pl., letters, learning.
γραφή, -ῆς, ἡ, indictment, prosecution.
γράφω, I write; mid., I indict, prosecute.
γυνή, γυναικός, ἡ, woman.

δαιμόνιον, -ου, τό, spirit, divine being.
δαίμων, -ονος, ὁ, god, divine being.
δάκρυ, -υος, τό, tear.
δακρύω, I weep, shed tears.
δέ, conj., but, and; μέν...δέ..., used to point a contrast between ideas.
δεῖ, δεήσει, it is necessary.
δείδω, δείσομαι, ἔδεισα, δέδια or δέδοικα, I fear.
δεινός, -ή, -όν, terrible, dangerous, strange; also with inf., clever at.
δέκα, ten.
δέομαι, δεήσομαι, ἐδεήθην, I need, beg, request.
δεσμός, -οῦ, ὁ, bond, fetter.
δεσμωτήριον, -ου, τό, prison.
δέχομαι, δέξομαι, ἐδεξάμην, I receive.
δεῦρο, adv., hither.
δέω, δεήσω, ἐδέησα, I want, lack, need.
δέω, δήσω, ἔδησα, I bind.

δή, particle of emphasis, indeed, then, in truth.
δῆλος, -η, -ον, clear, certain, evident.
δημιουργός, -οῦ, ὁ, craftsman, worker.
δημοκρατέομαι, I am under a democratic government.
δημόσιος, -α, -ον, public; δημοσίᾳ, as adv., in public.
δήπου, indef. adv., perhaps, I suppose.
δῆτα, adv., then, to be sure.
διά, prep., c. gen., through, by means of; c. acc., through, owing to.
διαβολή, -ῆς, ἡ, slander, prejudice.
διάγω, I pass, spend time.
διακινδυνεύω, I run every risk.
διαλέγομαι, I converse.
διαλείπω, I leave an interval, cease.
διανοέομαι, -νοήσομαι, -ενοήθην, I intend, purpose.
διάνοια, -ας, ἡ, thought, intention, meaning.
διαπειράομαι, I test thoroughly.
διατάττω, I set in order, arrange, post.
διατελέω, I bring to an end, or continue doing.
διατριβή, -ῆς, ἡ, spending of time, employment, discussion.
διατρίβω, I spend time, employ myself.
διαφερόντως, adv., differently.
διαφέρω, διοίσω, διήνεγκον, I differ from.
διαφθείρω, -φθερῶ, -έφθειρα, I harm, destroy, corrupt.
διδάσκω, I teach.
δίδωμι, I give.
διερωτάω, I cross-question.
διηγέομαι, I describe fully.
διημερεύω, I spend the day.
διθύραμβος, -ου, ὁ, dithyramb, lyric poetry.
δικάζω, I judge, give judgement.
δίκαιος, -α, -ον, just, right, lawful.

δικαίως, *adv.*, justly, rightly.
δικανικός, -ή, -όν, belonging to trials, relating to the law-courts.
δικαστήριον, -ου, τό, law-court.
δικαστής, -οῦ, ὁ, juryman.
δίκη, -ης, ἡ, law, an action, lawsuit; *also* penalty.
διοικέω, I manage.
δίς, twice.
δοκιμάζω, -άσω, I prove, approve.
δοκέω, δόξω, ἔδοξα, I think, seem, appear; *pass.*, τὸ δεδογμένον, that which seems good, is decided.
δόξα, -ης, ἡ, opinion, judgement, reputation.
δοξάζω, I think, judge.
δόσις, -εως, ἡ, gift.
δοῦλος, -ου, ὁ, slave.
δρᾶμα, -ατος, τό, act, action, performance.
δραχμή, -ῆς, ἡ, a drachma, *a coin worth a little less than a shilling.*
δράω, δράσω, I do, accomplish.
δύναμαι, δυνήσομαι, ἐδυνήθην, I am able, can.
δύναμις, -εως, ἡ, strength, power.
δυνατός, -ή, -όν, powerful, able, possible.
δύο, δυοῖν, two.
δυσμή, -ῆς, ἡ, setting, *of the sun.*

ἐάν, *conj.*, if.
ἑαυτόν, -οῦ, *reflex. pron.,3rd pers.*, himself.
ἐάω, I allow; ἐᾶν χαίρειν, to let alone, dismiss.
ἑβδομήκοντα, seventy.
ἐγγυάομαι, I pledge myself, go bail.
ἐγγυητής, -οῦ, ὁ, security, surety.
ἐγγύς, *adv.*, near.
ἐγείρω, ἐγερῶ, ἤγειρα, I rouse, waken.
ἐγκαλέω, I accuse, blame.
ἐγκαλύπτω, I hide, cover; *mid.*, I cover my face.

ἔγκλημα, -ατος, τό, charge, accusation.
ἐγώ, ἐμοῦ, μου, I, I myself.
ἐθέλω, -ήσω, I am willing.
ἐθίζω, ἐθιῶ, εἴθισα, I accustom.
εἰ, *condit. conj.*, if.
εἶεν, very well, well.
εἰκῆ, *adv.*, without heed, at random.
εἶμι (*fut.*), ᾖα, I shall go.
εἰμί, ἔσομαι, ἦν, I am; ἐστί, it is possible; τῷ ὄντι, in reality.
εἰρωνεύομαι, I say less than I mean, dissemble.
εἰς, *prep., c. acc.*, to, into, up to, until.
εἷς, μία, ἕν, one.
εἰσάγω, -άξω, -ήγαγον, I bring in, lead in, introduce.
εἰσέρχομαι, εἴσειμι, -ῆλθον, I go in, enter.
εἶτα, *adv.*, then.
εἴτε ... εἴτε ..., either ... or ..., whether ... or ...
εἴωθα (*perf. of* ἔθω), I am accustomed.
ἐκ, ἐξ, *prep., c. gen.*, from, out of.
ἕκαστος, -η, -ον, every, each.
ἑκάστοτε, *adv.*, each time.
ἐκβάλλω, -βαλῶ, -έβαλον, I throw out, reject.
ἐκεῖ, *adv.*, there.
ἐκεῖνος, -η, -ο (*demonst.*), that, he, she, it.
ἐκεῖσε, *adv.*, thither.
ἐκκαλύπτω, I uncover, reveal.
ἐκπίνω, -πίομαι, -έπιον, I drink, drain.
ἐκπλήσσω, -ξω, I frighten, amaze.
ἐκτίνω, I pay in full, pay.
ἐκτός, *adv.*, out of, outside.
ἐκτρέφω, -θρέψω, -έθρεψα, I bring up.
ἐκφεύγω, -φεύξομαι, I escape, am acquitted.
ἐκχέω, -χέω, I pour out, waste, throw away.
ἑκών, -οῦσα, -όν, willing, voluntary.

ἔλεγχος, -ου, ὁ, examination, test; ἔλεγχον διδόναι, to give an account of.

ἐλέγχω, I convince, disprove, reprove, examine.

ἐλεινός, -ή, -όν, pitiable.

ἐμαυτόν, -οῦ, reflex. pron., 1st pers., myself.

ἐμμελῶς, adv., regularly, agreeably.

ἐμμένω, -μενῶ, ἐνέμεινα, I abide by, continue.

ἐμός, -ή, -όν, my, mine.

ἐμποδών, adv., in the way, hindering.

ἔμπροσθε, adv., before, in front of.

ἐν, prep., c. dat., in, on, among.

ἐναντίος, -α, -ον, opposite, contrary.

ἐναντιόω, I place opposite; mid., I oppose, withstand.

ἐναργής, -ές, clear, distinct.

ἐνδεής, -ές, wanting, in need of.

ἔνδεκα, eleven; οἱ ἔνδεκα, the Athenian police-commissioners.

ἔνδον, adv., within.

ἕνεκα, on account of, with regard to.

ἐνέχω, I hold, keep fast; mid., ἐνέχομαι, I am liable to.

ἐνθάδε, adv., there, thither.

ἐνθένδε, adv., hence.

ἐνθουσιάζω, I am inspired.

ἐνιαυτός, -οῦ, ὁ, year.

ἐνίοτε, adv., sometimes, at times.

ἐνταῦθα, adv., there, then; also here, now.

ἐντεῦθεν, adv., thence, afterwards.

ἐντρέπω, I reprove; mid. and pass., I give heed to.

ἐνύπνιον, -ου, τό, dream.

ἐξαιρέομαι, -ελοῦμαι, -ειλόμην, I choose, take away, remove.

ἐξαμαρτάνω, I make a serious mistake.

ἐξανίστημι, -στήσω (trans.), -έστην, -έστηκα (intrans.), I make to rise up, I get up and depart.

ἐξαπατάω, I deceive.

ἐξελαύνω, -ελῶ, -ήλασα, I drive out, banish.

ἐξεργάζομαι, I accomplish, work out.

ἔξεστι, impers., it is allowed, possible.

ἐξετάζω, I question, examine closely, test.

ἐξουσία, -ας, ἡ, power, authority, means.

ἔοικα (perf. of εἴκω), I seem.

ἐπανέρχομαι, -ειμι, -ῆλθον, I go up, pass up, go back.

ἐπεγείρω, I awake, rouse.

ἐπεί, conj., when, since.

ἐπειδάν, conj., whenever.

ἐπειδή, conj., since.

ἐπέρχομαι, -ειμι, -ῆλθον, I come near, succeed, follow.

ἐπέχω, ἐφέξω, ἐπέσχον, I hold to, check, pause; mid., I keep hold of; ἐπέχω τὸν νοῦν, I turn my attention to.

ἐπί, prep., c. acc., to, on to, against; c. gen., upon, on, at; c. dat., in addition to, after.

ἐπιδείκνυμι, I show, point out.

ἐπιδημέω, I stay at home, am 'in town'.

ἐπιεικής, -ές, fitting, fair, reasonable.

ἐπιεικῶς, adv., fairly, probably, reasonably.

ἐπιθυμέω, I desire.

ἐπιθυμία, -ας, ἡ, desire, longing.

ἐπιλύω, I loose, release.

ἐπιμελέομαι, I take care of, give attention to.

ἐπινοέω, I think of, purpose, intend.

ἐπιορκέω, I swear falsely, break my oath.

ἐπιπέμπω, I send after, again.

ἐπισκοπέω, -σκέψομαι, -εσκεψάμην, I look upon, pay regard to, consider.

ἐπίσταμαι, -στήσομαι, ἠπιστήθην,
I know, understand.
ἐπιστάτης, -ου, ὁ, one set over,
manager, trainer.
ἐπιστέλλω, -στελῶ, -έστειλα, I
send to, bid, announce.
ἐπιστήμων, -ον, skilled in, learned.
ἐπιτάττω, -τάξω, I set over, put
in command, order.
ἐπιτήδειος, -α, -ον, serviceable,
necessary, friendly ; as subst.,
a near friend.
ἐπιτηδές, adv., for a special purpose, purposely.
ἐπιτίθημι, I put upon ; mid., I
set upon, attack.
ἐπιτρέπω, I hand over, entrust,
allow.
ἐπιτυγχάνω, -τεύξομαι, -έτυχον, I
light upon, reach, succeed in
doing.
ἐπίφθονος, -ον, jealous, malignant.
ἐπιχειρέω, I set my hand to, endeavour.
ἐπονείδιστος, -ον, disgraceful,
worthy of reproach.
ἔπος, ἔπεος, τό, word.
ἐργάζομαι, I do, perform, accomplish, work at.
ἔργον, -ου, τό, business, deed,
work ; ἔργῳ, in actual fact.
ἐρίβωλος, -ον, fertile.
ἔρομαι, ἐρήσομαι, ἠρόμην, I ask,
inquire.
ἔρχομαι, εἶμι, ἦλθον, I come, go.
ἐρῶ (fut. in use of φημί, λέγω),
εἶπον, εἴρηκα, I will say, tell.
ἐρωτάω, I ask, question.
ἑσπέρα, -ας, ἡ, evening.
ἑταῖρος, -ου, ὁ, comrade, companion.
ἑτοῖμος, -η, -ον, ready.
ἔτος, -εος, τό, year.
εὖ, adv., well.
εὐδαιμονία, -ας, ἡ, happiness.
εὐδαιμονίζω, I consider, pro-
nounce happy.
εὐδοκιμέω, I am esteemed, am
famous.

εὐειδής, -ές, graceful.
εὔελπις, -ι, hopeful, of good hope.
εὐεργετέω, I do well, confer bene-
fits.
Εὔηνος, -ου, ὁ, Evenus.
εὐθύς, adv., at once, immediately.
εὐκόλως, adv., calmly.
εὐμενῶς, adv., kindly, graciously.
εὑρίσκω, -ήσω, ηὗρον, I find, discover.
εὐσεβέω, I act reverently, piously.
εὐφημία, -ας, ἡ, use of words of
good omen, abstinence from
words of evil omen, solemn
silence.
εὐχερῶς, adv., cheerfully, without
disgust.
εὔχομαι, εὔξομαι, ηὐξάμην, I pray,
vow.
ἐφάπτομαι, I take hold of, touch.
ἐφεξῆς, adv., in order, in succes-
sion.
ἐφίημι, I let go, permit ; mid., I
earnestly beg, adjure.
Ἐχεκράτης, -ους, ὁ, Echecrates.
ἔχω, ἕξω or σχήσω, ἔσχον, I have,
possess, am able ; ἔχω with
adv., often = εἰμί with adj.,
e.g., ξένως ἔχω, I am strange
to ; ὥσπερ ἔχω ἔχειν, to be as
I am.
ἔωθεν, adv., from dawn, at day-
break.
ἕως, ἕω, ἡ, dawn, morning.

ζάω (fut. in use βιώσομαι), I
live.
Ζεύς, Διός, ὁ, Zeus.
ζητέω, I seek, inquire into, in-
vestigate.

ἤ, conj., or ; ἤ ... ἤ ..., either
... or ...
ἤ, interrog. particle. ἦ μήν, in
very truth, truly.
ἡβάω, -ήσω, ἥβησα, I am in the
prime of youth, early manhood.

ἡγέομαι, ἡγήσομαι, ἡγησάμην, I lead, consider, believe.
ἤδη, *adv.*, already, now.
ἡδέως, *adv.*, pleasantly, gladly.
ἥδιστος, -η, -ον, most pleasant, welcome; *superl. adv.*, ἥδιστα.
ἥκιστα, *adv.*, least.
ἥκω, ἥξω, I am come.
Ἠλεῖος, -α, -ον, of Elis.
ἡλικία, -ας, ἡ, age, time of life.
ἥλιος, -ου, ὁ, sun.
ἦμαρ, -ατος, τό, day; *poet. form of* ἡμέρα.
ἡμεῖς, -ῶν, we.
ἡμέρα, -ας, ἡ, day.
ἡμέτερος, -α, -ον, our.
ἠμί (*imperf.* 1st *and* 3rd *sing.*, ἦν, ἦ), I say.
ἡσυχῆ, *adv.*, silently, gently.
ἡσυχία, -ας, ἡ, peace, quiet; ἡσυχίαν ἄγω, I keep quiet.
ἦτρον, -ου, τό, stomach, belly.
ἥττων, -ον, less, worse, inferior.
ἠχή, -ῆς, ἡ, a confused noise, murmur.

θάνατος, -ου, ὁ, death.
θάπτω, I bury.
θάτερα = τὰ ἕτερα.
θαυμάζω, -άσω, ἐθαύμασα, I wonder, am astonished at, admire.
θαυμάσιος, -α, -ον, wonderful, marvellous; ὣ θαυμάσιε, my dear sir!
θεμιτός, -ή, -όν, lawful, right.
θεόμαντις, -εως, ὁ, a man inspired, a prophet.
θεός, -οῦ, ὁ, God, a god.
θεωρία, -ας, ἡ, a sight, spectacle; the sending of θεωροί *or* state-ambassadors *to an oracle or the games*, a mission.
Θησεύς, -έως, ὁ, Theseus.
θνήσκω, θανοῦμαι, ἔθανον, τέθνηκα, I die.
θόλος, -ου, ὁ, dome, vault; the round chamber *at Athens where the Prytanes dined.*
θορυβέω, I make an uproar.

θυρωρός, -οῦ, ὁ, doorkeeper, porter.
ἱερεύς, -έως, ὁ, priest.
ἱκανός, -ή, -όν, befitting, sufficient, considerable.
ἱκανῶς, *adv.*, sufficiently, enough.
ἱκνέομαι, ἵξομαι, ἱκόμην, I come to, reach.
ἱμάτιον, -ου, τό, cloak; *pl.*, clothes.
ἵνα, *conj.*, that, in order that; *adv.*, where.
Ἱππίας, -ου, ὁ, Hippias.
ἱππικός, -ή, -όν, concerned with horses, skilled in horsemanship.
Ἱππόνικος, -ου, ὁ, Hipponicus.
ἵππος, -ου, ὁ, horse.
Ἰσθμός, -οῦ, ὁ, the Isthmus of Corinth.
ἵστημι, στήσω, ἔστησα, I set up; ἔστην, ἔστηκα (*intrans.*), I stand.
ἰσχυρός, -ά, -όν, strong, powerful.
ἴσως, *adv.*, perhaps.
ἰτέον (*verb. adj. of* εἶμι), one must go.
ἴχνος, -εος, τό, track, footstep.

καθάπτομαι, I lay hold on, accost, upbraid.
καθαρεύω, I am clean, pure.
καθέζομαι, καθεδοῦμαι, I sit down.
καθεύδω, -ήσω, I sleep.
κάθημαι, I am seated, sit.
καθίστημι, I make, render, bring into a state of.
καθομολογέω, I confess.
καί, *conj.*, and, also, even.
καὶ γάρ, *conj.*, for surely.
καὶ δή, *conj.*, and even, and indeed; καὶ δὴ καί, and besides, moreover.
καινός, -ή, -όν, new, fresh.
καιρός, -οῦ, ὁ, the right time.
καίτοι, *conj.*, and yet.
κακουργέω, I do evil, hurt, harm.
κακός, -ή, -όν, bad, evil, wrong, wicked.

κακῶς, *adv.*, ill, badly; κακῶς
ποιέω, I ill-treat, do wrong to.
καλέω, καλῶ, ἐκάλεσα, I call.
Καλλίας, -ου, ὁ, Callias.
καλλιεπέω, I speak elegantly.
καλλύνω, I adorn; *mid.*, I pride
myself.
καλλωπίζω, I beautify; *mid.*, I
adorn myself, make a display,
glory in.
καλός, -ή, -όν, fair, good, right,
noble; *comp.*, καλλίων, -ον;
superl., κάλλιστος, -η, -ον.
καλῶς, *adv.*, well, nobly.
καρδία, -ας, ἡ, heart.
καρτερέω, I endure bravely.
κατά, *prep.*, *c. gen.*, down upon,
against; *c. acc.*, concerning,
according to, throughout.
καταγέλαστος, -ον, ridiculous.
καταγελάω, I laugh at, mock.
καταγιγνώσκω, -γνώσομαι, -έγνων,
I give sentence, condemn.
κατάδηλος, -ον, plain, manifest.
κατακλάω, -κλάσω, -έκλασα, I break
down, overcome.
κατακλίνω, I lay down; *pass.*, I
lie down.
καταλαμβάνω, -λήψομαι, -έλαβον,
I seize, catch, discover.
καταλείπω, I leave behind, give up.
καταλύω, I make an end of.
καταράομαι, I curse.
καταφρονέω, I scorn, despise.
καταχαρίζομαι, I do a favour.
καταψηφίζομαι, I vote against, in
condemnation of.
κατέχω, I restrain.
κατηγορέω, I charge, accuse.
κατήγορος, -ου, ὁ, accuser.
Κεῖος, -α, -ον, Ceian, from the
island of Ceos.
κελεύω, I command, bid, urge.
κεν, *Ionic form of* ἄν.
κήδομαι, I am distressed, anxious.
κινδυνεύω, I run risks, venture,
am likely to.
κίνδυνος, -ου, ὁ, danger, risk, peril.
κινέω, I move, set in motion.

Κλαζομένιος, -α, -ον, of Clazomenae.
κλάω, κλαύσομαι, ἔκλαυσα, I weep,
lament.
κνήμη, -ης, ἡ, shin, leg.
κοινῇ, *adv.*, in common.
κοινός, -ή, -όν, common.
κοινωνέω, I have a share in.
κολούω, I curtail, cut short, restrain.
κοσμέω, I arrange, set in order,
embellish.
κορυβαντιάω, I celebrate the rites
of the Corybantes, *the priests
of Cybele.*
Κρήτη, -ης, ἡ, the island of Crete.
κρίνω, κρινῶ, ἔκρινα, I judge, ar-
raign, try.
Κριτόβουλος, -ου, ὁ, Critobulus.
Κρίτων, -ωνος, ὁ, Crito.
κρούω, κρούσω, ἔκρουσα, I strike, hit.
κτῆσις, -εως, ἡ, possession.
κύριος, -α, -ον, having power, authority.
κύων, κυνός, ὁ, dog.

λαμβάνω, λήψομαι, ἔλαβον, I take,
get.
λανθάνω, λήσω, ἔλαθον, I escape
notice, do something secretly.
λέγω, λέξω, I say, speak, tell,
refer to, mean.
λείπω, λείψω, ἔλιπον, I leave,
desert.
λέξις, -εως, ἡ, speech, way of
speaking.
Λεοντῖνος, -η, -ον, of Leontini in
Sicily.
λευκός, -ή, -όν, white.
Λέων, -οντος, ὁ, Leon.
λίαν, *adv.*, too much.
λίθος, -ου, ὁ, stone.
λογίζομαι, I reckon, calculate, reason.
λόγος, -ου, ὁ, word, conversation,
discussion, speech.
λοιπός, -ή, -όν, left, remaining.
λούω, I wash; *mid. and pass.*,
I wash myself, bathe.

λυπέω, distress, grieve.
λύπη, -ης, ή, pain, grief.
λυσιτελέω, I am useful, advantageous.
λύω, I loose, release.
λῷστος, -η, -ον, best.

μά, particle used in oaths of strong protestation, e.g., μὰ Δία.
μακαρίζω, I call happy, bless.
μακάριος, -α, -ον, blessed, happy, fortunate.
μάλα, adv., very, very much, exceedingly; comp., μᾶλλον; superl., μάλιστα; ἐν τοῖς μάλιστα, as much as any.
μανθάνω, μαθήσομαι, ἔμαθον, I learn, ascertain, understand.
μαντεία, -ας, ή, oracle.
μαντεύομαι, I prophesy.
μάρτυς, μάρτυρος, ὁ, witness.
μάτην, adv., in vain, foolishly.
μέγας, μεγάλη, μέγα, great, powerful, important; comp., μείζων, -ον; superl., μέγιστος, -η, -ον.
μέγεθος, -εος, τό, size.
μειράκιον, -ου, τό, a lad, stripling.
μέλει, impers., it is a care to, the concern of.
Μέλητος, -ου, ὁ, Meletus.
μέλλω, I am about to, intend, am likely to.
μέμφομαι, I blame, reproach.
μέν, particle, followed generally by δέ, the two serving to point a contrast between words or clauses.
μὲν δή, however.
μέντοι, at any rate, yet, nevertheless.
μένω, μενῶ, ἔμεινα, I stay, remain, await.
μέρος, -εος, τό, part, portion, share.
μετά, prep., c. acc., after, according to; c. gen., with, among.
μεταδίδωμι, I give a share of.
μεταξύ, adv. and prep. (c. gen.), between.

μεταπέμπομαι, I send for.
μεταστρέφω, I turn round.
μετοικέω, I change my place of residence, go away.
μετριώτατα, adv., most moderately.
μή, not, lest; used normally in dependent clauses, where the negation is of something other than a simple assertion.
μηδαμῶς, adv., in no way.
μηδέ, adv., nor, not even.
μηδείς, μηδεμία, μηδέν, no one, nothing; μηδέν as adv., not at all.
μήτε ... μήτε ..., neither ... nor ...
μικρός, -ά, -όν, small, little.
μισθόω, I let out on hire; mid., I hire, engage.
μνᾶ, μνᾶς, ή, mina, a sum of money about £4.
μόνος, -η, -ον, alone, only.
μορμολύττομαι, I scare, frighten.
μύωψ, -ωπος, ὁ, gadfly, horse-fly.

ναί, adv. of strong affirmation, yes, verily.
ναυμαχία, -ας, ή, sea-fight.
νεκρός, -οῦ, ὁ, dead body, corpse; also adj., νεκρός, -ά, -όν.
νέος, -α, -ον, young, new; οἱ νέοι, young men.
νεότης, -ητος, ή, spirit of youth, rashness.
νεώτερος, -α, -ον, younger.
νή, particle of strong affirmation, with acc. of person invoked.
νομίζω, I think, consider, believe in.
νόμος, -ου, ὁ, custom, law.
νοῦς, νοῦ, ὁ, mind.
νῦν, νυνί, adv., now.
νυνδή, adv., now indeed.
νυστάζω, I nod, slumber, 'take a nap'.
νωθέστερος, -α, -ον, rather sluggish, lazy.

Ξανθίππη, -ης, ἡ, Xanthippe, *wife of Socrates.*

ξένος, -ου, ὁ, stranger, foreigner.

ξένως, *adv.,* strangely; ξένως ἔχω, I am a stranger to.

ξυγχωρέω, I give way, concede.

ὁ, ἡ, τό, *dej. art.,* the.

ὅδε, ἥδε, τόδε (*demonst. pron.*), this, the following.

οἶδα, ᾔδη, εἰδέναι (*perf. of* εἴδω), I know.

οἴκαδε, *adv.,* homeward.

οἰκεῖος, -α, -ον, akin; οἱ οἰκεῖοι, friends, relatives.

οἴομαι, οἰήσομαι, ᾠήθην, I think, suppose.

οἷος, -α, -ον, of what kind, like; οἷός τ' εἰμί, I am able to.

οἷόσπερ, -απερ, -όνπερ, *strengthened form of* οἷος.

οἴχομαι, I am gone, go off.

ὀλιγαρχία, -ας, ἡ, oligarchy.

ὀλίγος, -η, -ον, little, small, few; ὀλίγου, *as adv.,* within a little, almost; ἐν ὀλίγῳ, in short.

ὅλος, -η, -ον, whole, entire.

ὄμμα, -ατος, τό, eye.

ὄμνυμι, ὀμοῦμαι, ὤμοσα, I swear.

ὅμοιος, -α, -ον, like.

ὁμολογέω, I agree with, admit.

ὁμολογία, -ας, ἡ, agreement, compact, admission.

ὅμως, *adv.,* nevertheless.

ὀνειδίζω, I reproach, upbraid.

ὀνίνημι, ὀνήσω, ὤνησα, I profit, benefit; *mid.,* I have profit in, thrive.

ὄνομα, -ατος, τό, name, expression, term.

ὅπη, *adv.,* where; ὁπηοῦν, wherever.

ὅποι, *adv.,* whither.

ὁπότερος, -α, -ον, which of two.

ὅπως, *conj.,* how, that, in order that.

ὁπωστιοῦν, *adv.,* in any respect.

ὁράω, ὄψομαι, εἶδον, ἑώρακα, I see.

ὀρθότης, -ητος, ἡ, rightness, fitness.

ὄρθρος, -ου, ὁ, dawn.

ὀρθῶς, *adv.,* rightly, justly, truly.

ὀρχήστρα, -ας, ἡ, orchestra, *the space in front of the Greek stage given up to the chorus.*

ὅς, ἥ, ὅ, *relat. pron.,* who, which; used also as demonst. pron., = οὗτος, ὅδε, this, he.

ὅσιος, -α, -ον, sacred; devout, religious.

ὅσος, -η, -ον, how great, how much, how many.

ὅσπερ, ἥπερ, ὅπερ, *strengthened form of relat. pron.*

ὅστις, ἥτις, ὅτι, who, whoever.

ὅταν, *adv.,* when, whenever.

ὅτε, *adv.,* when.

ὅτι, *conj.,* that, because.

οὐ, οὐκ, οὐχί, not; *negative of actual assertions.*

οὗ, *adv.,* where.

οὐδαμοῦ, *adv.,* nowhere.

οὐδαμόσε, *adv.,* to no place.

οὐδαμῶς, *adv.,* in no wise.

οὐδέ, nor, not even.

οὐδείς, οὐδεμία, οὐδέν, no one, nothing; οὐδέν *as adv.,* not at all; οὐδεὶς ὅστις οὐ, every one.

οὐδέποτε, *adv.,* never.

οὐδέτερος, -ον, neither of two.

οὐκέτι, *adv.,* no longer.

οὔκουν, *adv.,* not then.

οὐκοῦν, *adv.,* then, therefore.

οὖν, *adv.,* then, therefore, so.

οὔτε, and not; οὔτε ... οὔτε ..., neither ... nor ...

οὔτοι, *adv.,* indeed not.

οὗτος, αὕτη, τοῦτο, this.

οὕτω, οὕτως, *adv.,* thus; *strengthened form* οὑτωσί.

ὀφείλω, I owe.

ὀφθαλμός, -οῦ, ὁ, eye.

πάθος, -εος, τό, experience, suffering.

παιδεύω, I teach, instruct, educate.

παιδιά, -ᾶς, ἡ, child's play, game.
παιδίον, -ου, τό, child.
παίζω, I jest, trifle.
παῖς, παιδός, ὁ, child, son, youth.
πάλαι, adv., long ago, of old, formerly.
πάλιν, adv., back, again.
παντάπασι, adv., wholly, altogether.
πανταχοῦ, adv., everywhere.
πάντως, adv., wholly, altogether.
πάνυ, adv., altogether, very, very much; in answers, certainly.
παρά, prep., c. acc., beyond, contrary to, in comparison with; c. gen., from; c. dat., by, at.
παραβαίνω, I go beyond, transgress.
παραγγέλλω, I pass word, announce, bid.
παρακάθημαι, I sit beside.
παρακρούω, I mislead.
παραμένω, I stand by, remain with, endure.
παραμυθέομαι, I encourage, console.
παρανόμως, adv., contrary to law, unconstitutionally.
παράπαν, adv., on the whole, altogether.
παρασκευάζω, I prepare.
πάρειμι, -έσομαι, I am present.
παρέρχομαι, -ειμι, -ῆλθον, I go by, pass, come to, come forward.
παρέχω, I supply, afford; mid., I offer, bring forward.
παρίημι, I let go; mid., I beg off, beseech, ask pardon.
Πάριος, -α, -ον, from the island of Paros.
παρίστημι, I set beside; intrans. tenses, to be at hand, present.
πᾶς, πᾶσα, πᾶν, all, every.
πάσχω, πείσομαι, ἔπαθον, πέπονθα, I suffer, experience.
πατήρ, πατρός, ὁ, father.
πατρίς, -ίδος, ἡ, native country.
παύω, I stop, bring to an end; mid., I cease, leave off.

πείθω, I persuade; mid. and pass., I am persuaded, obey.
πειράομαι, I try; I make trial of, test, experience.
πέμπω, I send.
πέμπτος, -η, -ον, fifth; πέμπτος αὐτός, with four others.
πέντε, five.
περί, prep., c. acc., about; c. gen., about, on account of; c. dat., round about, for.
περιάπτω, I fasten about, attach to.
περιγίγνομαι, -γενήσομαι, -εγενόμην, I prevail over, am superior to, survive.
περιέρχομαι, -ειμι, -ῆλθον, I go round, go about.
περιμένω, I wait for, await.
πῃ, adv., somehow.
πήγνυμι, I fix; pass., I become stiff.
πηνίκα, adv., at what point of time?
πιέζω, πιέσω, ἐπίεσα, I press, squeeze.
πίνω, πίομαι, ἔπιον, πέπωκα, I drink.
πιστεύω, I believe, trust in.
πλάνη, -ης, ἡ, wandering.
πλάττω, I mould, make up, fabricate.
Πλάτων, -ωνος, ὁ, Plato.
πλείων, -ον, or πλέων, -ον, more.
πλεῖστος, -η, -ον, very much, very great, greatest.
πλημμέλεια, -ας, ἡ, fault, error.
πλημμελέω, I err, offend.
πλημμελής, -ές, in fault, error.
πλήν, adv. and prep., beyond, except.
πλησίον, adv., near, hard by.
πλοῖον, -ου, τό, ship.
ποδαπός, -ή, -όν, from what country?
πόθεν, adv., whence?
ποιέω, ποιήσω, I make, compose; mid., I hold, reckon, esteem; περὶ πλείονος, πλείστου ποιοῦμαι, I reckon more, most highly.

ποίημα, -ατος, τό, work, poetical work, poem.
ποίησις, -εως, ἡ, a poem.
ποιητής, -οῦ, ὁ, a maker, poet.
πόλις, -εως, ἡ, city, state.
πολιτεύομαι, I live in a state.
πολίτης, -ου, ὁ, citizen.
πολιτικός, -ή, -όν, of or befitting a citizen, belonging to the state, public; ὁ πολιτικός, as *subst.*, a statesman.
πολλάκις, *adv.*, often.
πολύς, πολλή, πολύ, many, much; πολύ as *adv.*, much, *e.g.*, πολὺ μᾶλλον, much more.
πονέω, I toil, labour, work hard.
πονηρός, -ά, -όν, painful, bad, worthless, wicked.
πόνος, -ου, ὁ, toil, hard work.
πόσος, -η, -ον, how much? how great? of what value?
πότε, *adv.*, when?
πότερος, -α, -ον, which of two? πότερον and πότερα, as *adv.*, whether?
Ποτείδαια, -ας, ἡ, Potidaea, a town in Chalcidice.
που, *enclitic particle*, somewhere, anywhere.
πούς, ποδός, ὁ, foot.
πρᾶγμα, -ατος, τό, deed, matter, affair; *pl.*, affairs, business.
πραγματεύομαι, I am busy; *perf. pass.*, πεπραγματεῦσθαι, to be worked at, laboured at.
πρακτέος, -α, -ον, to be done.
πρᾶος, -εία, -ον, mild, gentle; *comp.*, πρᾳότερος, -α, -ον.
πράττω, πράξω, ἔπραξα, I do, accomplish, manage; χρήματα πράττω, I exact money, *also* mid., *in same sense.*
πράως, *adv.*, gently.
πρέπει, *impers.*, it is fitting, becomes.
πρεσβεύω, I put first, honour.
πρεσβύτερος, -α, -ον, elder.
πρίαμαι, ἐπριάμην, I buy.
πρίν, *adv.*, before.

πρό, *prep.*, c. *gen.*, before, instead of.
προαγορεύω, I foretell.
Πρόδικος, -ου, ὁ, Prodicus.
προθυμέομαι, I am eager, earnest.
προθυμία, -ας, ἡ, readiness, zeal, goodwill.
προῖκα, *adv.*, freely, for nothing.
προκρίνω, I prefer, judge beforehand.
πρός, *prep.*, c. *acc.*, to, against, in answer to, relating to; c. *gen.*, in presence of, before, ' in the name of'; c. *dat.*, besides.
προσδοκάω, I expect, look for.
προσέρχομαι, -ειμι, -ῆλθον, I come to, draw near.
προσερῶ (*fut.*), I will address, speak to.
προσήκων, -ουσα, -ον, belonging to, befitting, akin.
πρόσθεν, *adv.*, before, formerly.
προσκαθίζω, I sit down by.
πρόσκειμαι, I am placed upon, attached to, press upon; *of things*, to be imposed, inflicted upon.
πρόσοιδα, I know besides; χάριν πρόσοιδα, I owe thanks besides.
προσποιοῦμαι, I gain over, lay claim to, affect.
προστάσσω, I place, post; appoint, give orders.
προστίθημι, -θήσω, -έθηκα, I put to, apply, bestow upon, inflict.
προτεραῖος, -α, -ον, of the day before; as *subst.*, ἡ προτεραία, the day before.
πρότερος, -α, -ον, before, earlier; πρότερον as *adv.*, before, sooner.
προτίθημι, I set out, present, propose, set forth.
πρύμνα, -ης, ἡ, stern *of a ship.*
πρυτανεύω, I am president, hold office as Prytanis.
πρύτανις, -εως, ὁ, a Prytanis, pre-

VOCABULARY

110   VOCABULARY

sident, a member of the committee of the Council.
πρώ, *adv.*, early; *comp.*, πρωαίτερον; *superl.*, πρωαίτατα.
πρῶτος, -η, -ον, first, foremost; πρῶτον as *adv.*, in the first place, first.
πυνθάνομαι, πεύσομαι, ἐπυθόμην, I ask, learn, ascertain.
πῶλος, -ου, ὁ, foal, colt.
πώποτε, ever yet.
πῶς, *adv.*, how? πως, *enclitic adv.*, in any way, at all.

ῥᾳδίως, *adv.*, easily; *comp.*, ῥᾷον; *superl.*, ῥᾷστα.
ῥᾷστος, -η, -ον, easiest.
ῥῆμα, -ατος, τό, word, saying, phrase.
ῥητέον, *verb. adj.*, one must say.
ῥήτωρ, -ορος, ὁ, public speaker, orator, rhetorician.

Σαλαμίνιος, -α, -ον, from Salamis.
Σαλαμίς, -ῖνος, ἡ, the island of Salamis.
σαφής, -ές, clear, plain, certain.
σαφῶς, *adv.*, clearly, surely; *comp.*, σαφέστερον.
σεαυτόν, -οῦ, *reflex. pron.*, 2nd *pers.*, yourself.
σελήνη, -ης, ἡ, moon.
σημεῖον, -ου, τό, sign, token; *the* divine 'sign' *of Socrates*.
σιγάω, I am silent, keep silence.
σιγῇ, *adv.*, in silence, silently.
σκέλος, -εος, τό, leg.
σκοπέω, σκέψομαι, ἐσκεψάμην, I look at, consider, pay regard to, inquire.
σός, σή, σόν, your (*sing.*).
Σούνιον, -ου, τό, Sunium, *the southern promontory of Attica.*
σοφία, -ας, ἡ, wisdom.
σοφιστής, -οῦ, ὁ, a wise man, professional teacher, sophist.
σοφός, -ή, -όν, wise; *comp.*, σοφώτερος; *superl.*, σοφώτατος.

σπουδάζω, -άσομαι, ἐσπούδασα, I am zealous, earnest.
σπουδή, *adv.*, in earnest, seriously.
στερέω, I deprive.
στέφω, -ψω, ἔστεψα, I crown.
στόμα, -ατος, τό, mouth.
στρατεύομαι, I serve as a soldier.
στρατηγός, -οῦ, ὁ, general, commander.
σύ, σοῦ, you (*sing.*).
συγγιγνώσκω, -γνώσομαι, -έγνων, I make allowances for, pardon.
συλλαμβάνω, -λήψομαι, -έλαβον, I put together, close; I lay hold of, arrest.
συλλέγομαι, I assemble.
συμβαίνω, -βήσομαι, -έβην, I agree with, suit, fit; *of things*, to happen, turn out.
σύμπας, -πασα, -παν, all together, all.
συμφορά, -ᾶς, ἡ, event, circumstance, misfortune.
συνδοκεῖ, *impers.*, it is agreed.
σύνειμι, -έσομαι, I am with, am engaged with.
συνήθης, -ες, well-acquainted, familiar.
συνθήκη, -ης, ἡ, agreement, covenant, contract.
σύνοιδα, I am cognizant of, am conscious.
συνουσία, -ας, ἡ, intercourse, association, society.
συντίθημι, -θήσω, -έθηκα, I put together, construct, contrive.
σφεῖς, σφᾶς, σφῶν, they.
σφόδρα, *adv.*, very much, exceedingly, vehemently.
σχεδόν, *adv.*, near, nearly.
σώζω, σώσω, ἔσωσα, I save, keep, observe; *pass.*, I escape.
Σωκράτης, -ους, ὁ, Socrates.

τάξις, -εως, ἡ. rank, post, position.
τάσσω, -ξω, ἔταξα, I put in order, post, station, give orders.

ταύτῃ, adv., in this way.
τάχ' ἄν, probably, perhaps.
ταχύς, -εῖα, -ύ, quick, swift.
τεκμαίρομαι, I infer, conclude.
τεκμήριον, -ου, τό, sign, token, proof.
τελευταῖος, -α, -ον, last.
τελευτάω, I bring to an end, I die.
τελευτή, -ῆς, ἡ, end, fulfilment.
τελέω, I complete, accomplish; I pay, spend.
τέτταρες, -ων, four.
τέχνη, -ης, ἡ, art, skill, craft, trade.
τέως, adv., for a time, so long, ere this.
τηλικόσδε, -ήδε, -όνδε }
τηλικοῦτος, -αύτη, -οῦτο } so much, so great, so old.
τήμερον, adv., to-day.
τηνικάδε, adv., at this time of day, so early.
τιμάω, I honour, respect, reward; also I estimate, and mid., assess a penalty.
τιμωρέω, I avenge; mid., I take vengeance, punish.
τιμωρία, -ας, ἡ, help, vengeance, punishment.
τις, τι, indef., one, some one, any one, something.
τίς, τί, interrog., who? what?
τοι, enclitic particle, so, in truth.
τοιοῦτος, -αύτη, -οῦτο, of such a kind.
τοσοῦτος, -αύτη, -οῦτο }
and -οῦτον } so great, so much,
τοσόσδε, -ήδε, -όνδε }
τότε, adv., then.
τραγῳδία, -ας, ἡ, tragedy.
τράπεζα, -ης, ἡ, table, money-changer's counter.
τρέφω, θρέψω, ἔθρεψα, τέτροφα, I nourish, bring up.
τριάκοντα, thirty.
τρίβω, I spend, pass (of time).
τρίτατος, -η, -ον, third (poet. form).

τριχῇ, adv., threefold.
τρόπος, -ου, ὁ, fashion, manner, way of life, habit, custom.
τροφεύς, -έως, ὁ, one who brings up, foster-parent.
τυγχάνω, τεύξομαι, ἔτυχον, I light upon, meet, get, obtain; also intrans., to happen to be, befall, come to pass.
τύχη, -ης, ἡ, chance, fortune (either good or bad).
ὕβρις, -εως, ἡ, insolence, licentiousness.
ὑβριστής, -οῦ, ὁ, one who is violent and overbearing.
υἱός, -οῦ, also υἱέος or υέος, son.
ὑμεῖς, -ῶν, you.
ὑμέτερος, -α, -ον, your.
ὑπακούω, I listen to and answer, answer a knock on the door, obey, submit.
ὑπείκω, -είξω, -εῖξα and -είκαθον, retire from, withdraw, yield.
ὑπέρ, prep., c. acc., beyond, contrary to; c. gen., over, on behalf of, for the sake of.
ὑπηρέτης, -ου, ὁ, assistant, servant.
ὑποδέχομαι, -δέξομαι, -εδεξάμην, I entertain, undertake, admit, wait for.
ὑπολαμβάνω, -λήψομαι, -έλαβον, I overtake, take up an idea, entice, draw away.
ὑπολογίζομαι, -ιοῦμαι, I take into consideration.
ὑποστέλλω, -στελῶ, -έστειλα, I draw back, conceal, dissemble.
ὕπτιος, -α, -ον, on the back.
ὕστατον, adv., last, at last.
ὑστεραία, ἡ (sc. ἡμέρα), following, next day.
ὕστερος, -α, -ον, coming after, following, later; ὕστερον as adv., afterwards.
ὑφηγέομαι, I guide, lead the way.
φαίνομαι, φανοῦμαι, ἐφάνην, I appear, seem; with inf., I appear to be; with part., I clearly am.

φάρμακον, -ου, τό, medicine, drug.
φάσκω, I say.
φαῦλος, -η, -ον, slight, trivial, worthless, bad.
φείδομαι, φείσομαι, ἐφεισάμην, I spare.
φέρω, οἴσω, ἤνεγκα, I bear, carry, bring; endure or suffer; win, gain, achieve.
φεύγω, φεύξομαι, ἔφυγον, I flee, shrink from, avoid; go into exile; am prosecuted at law.
φημί, ἔφην, I say, tell; also I say yes, assent.
φθέγγομαι, I utter.
Φθία, -ας, Ep. Φθίη, ἡ, Phthia, a district in Thessaly.
φιλόπολις, -εως, ὁ, patriot.
φίλος, -η, -ον, dear; as subst., friend.
φιλοσοφέω, I seek after knowledge, pursue wisdom.
φιλοψυχία, -ας, ἡ, excessive love of life, cowardice.
φλυαρία, -ας, ἡ, foolish talk, nonsense.
φοβέομαι, -ήσομαι, ἐφοβήθην, I am frightened, fear.
φοιτάω, I go constantly to, resort to, go to and fro.
φορτικός, -ή, -όν, tiresome, vulgar, commonplace.
φρόνιμος, -η, -ον, sensible, sober, prudent; adv., φρονίμως.
φυγή, -ῆς, ἡ, flight, escape, banishment.
φύλαξ, -ακος, ὁ, watcher, guard, keeper.
φυλή, -ῆς, ἡ, tribe.
φύσις, -εως, ἡ, nature.
φωνή, -ῆς, ἡ, voice, language, dialect.

χαίρω, I rejoice, take pleasure in; I hail, also bid farewell to.

χαλεπαίνω, I am angry, embittered.
χαλεπός, -ή, -όν, grievous, difficult, troublesome, harsh, angry.
χαριεντίζομαι, I am witty, jest.
χαρίζομαι, I show favour.
χάρις, -ιτος, ἡ, favour, goodwill, kindness.
χειροτέχνης, -ου, ὁ, craftsman, artisan.
χείρων, -ον, worse, inferior.
χρή, ἔχρην and χρῆν, it is necessary, right.
χρῆμα, -ατος, τό (mostly pl.), goods, money; affairs, business, event.
χρησμός, -οῦ, ὁ, the answer of an oracle, oracle.
χρησμῳδέω, I prophesy.
χρησμῳδός, -οῦ, ὁ, prophet, soothsayer.
χρηστός, -ή, -όν, useful, favourable, auspicious, good.
χρόνος, -ου, ὁ, time, time of life.
χωρέω, I give way, retire; I advance, go on; of things, to turn out, succeed.
χωρίς, adv. and prep., apart, apart from.

ψεύδομαι, I lie, cheat, deceive.
ψηφίζομαι, -ιοῦμαι, ἐψηφισάμην, I vote, decide by vote, resolve.
ψύχω, I make cold; pass., I grow cold.

ὤ, exclam., oh!
ὧδε, adv., so, thus.
ὥρα, -ας, ἡ, time.
ὥς, adv., so, thus.
ὡς, conj., as, when, that, how; also used to strengthen superl., like Latin quam, e.g. ὡς πλεῖστοι, as many as possible.
ὥσπερ, adv., just as.
ὥστε, conj., so that, so as to.